The Must of the Matter

REVEREND

Jerry D. Black

Published by Hardnett Publishing®
© Copyright 2006 | Reverend Jerry D. Black
All Rights Reserved

No part of this book may be reproduced or transmitted in any form or by any means, electronic or mechanical, including photocopying and recording, or by any information storage or retrieval system, except as may be expressly permitted in writing by the publisher. Requests for permission should be addressed in writing to Hardnett Publishing®; P.O. Box 80575 Conyers, Georgia 30013

ISBN 10: 0-9789310-0-9
ISBN 13: 978-0-9789310-0-1

Unless otherwise noted, Scripture quotations are from the
Holy Bible, King James Version

Printed in the United States of America

Hardnett Publishing®
P.O. Box 80575
Conyers, Georgia 30013

With joy and much thanks,

I dedicate this book to my loving wife of over 30 years,

Mrs. Glenda J. Black,

and our four wonderful children,

Tangie, Jerry, Jr., Erica and Terica.

Table of Contents

Preface xi

Part One: The *Must* of Salvation 1

The Must of the Matter 3
The Middle Man 13
Stories of the Lost and Found 19
Don't Turn This Invitation Down 31

Part Two: The *Must* of Prayer and Faith 39

Miracles 42
Can God be Trusted? 49
Crucial Faith for Critical Times 57
A Faith that Will not Quit 64
The Awesome Power of Prayer 71

Part Three: The *Must* of Victorious Living 81

The Importance of Right Choices 84
Check Your Crowd 90
The Wolf Country 97
Going to Another Level 105

Part Four: The *Must* of Embracing
Our God-given Destinies 113

    The Race that is Set Before Us. 116
    The Almighty God. 123
    Coping with the Cup 130
    Still Wanted by the Lord 139

Part Five: The *Must* of Praising God 147

    The Reason I Love Him. 149
    Thanks in Everything. 159
    Passionate Praise 166

ACKNOWLEDGMENTS

I am indeed grateful for each expression of God's love and favor without which my journey would have been impossible. I am also grateful for the love and discipline of my late grandmother, my late father, and my mother, Mrs. Helen Brewer.

I owe a tremendous debt of gratitude to my wonderful wife, Mrs. Glenda Black, and our four children, Tangie, Jerry, Jr., Erica and Terica, who across the years have been a source of joy and support. Thank you to my Beulah Baptist family, and my close friends for many years, Reverend Maurice Watson and Reverend William L. Robinson.

Lastly, special thanks to Mrs. Felicia Hardnett for all of your help and assistance with this project.

God bless you all!!

FOREWORD

I met Reverend Black many years ago when he was pastoring the Greater Paradise Baptist Church in Little Rock, Arkansas. Over the years, I have come to know him as a minister of integrity with a keen sense of social justice. He stands in the ranks of those who hear the prophet's call to do justice, to be merciful, and to walk humbly before God. It is spiritual leaders such as these who have made a tremendous impact on American society, and on the world. Where would America be without Dr. Martin Luther King, Jr., Dr. Samuel Proctor, Rev. William Sloan Coffin, Jr. and so many others who, behind the scenes or in front news cameras have demanded justice and equality and peace. Where would America be without the demands that led to the Voting Rights Act of 1965? Where would the world be without the demands to end *apartheid* in South Africa? We would still be walking in darkness, seeing only a faint glimmer of hope. The role of inspired spiritual leaders like Reverend Black continues to be to inspire hope, AND to be in the front ranks of direct action movements.

We live our lives in faith, but under the law. Therefore we must continue to struggle for justice and compassionate laws. We must strengthen our spiritual resolve, and live our everyday lives in such a way that we seek justice, do acts of mercy, and humbly give our lives to God.

Pastor Black is very well-known among clergy and is sought after as a preacher at ministerial conventions. He is a master orator who builds his sermons on a solid base of Biblical scholarship. His sermons are spiritually uplifting and illuminating, encouraging all of us to live our lives in the light of God's Word.

The Must of the Matter comes at a critical time in our nation's spiritual evolution. It seems that our nation's political leadership has forgotten the needs of the poor, the homeless, and the ill who need medical care. They have replaced compassion with tax-breaks for their friends. They have exchanged diplomacy for an unjustified war based on fiction, not facts. In this climate, we welcome a message of living our lives in the light of God, in the footsteps of Jesus and the prophets. The spiritual truths set forth in *The Must of the Matter* serve as a clarion call to every believer to live out their faith every day and in every area of their lives. As believers, we would do well to read this important piece during our study time and allow the Spirit of the Lord to transform our hearts and minds and make us fit for service.

Reverend Jesse L. Jackson, Sr.
Founder and President
Rainbow PUSH Coalition
June 2006

PREFACE

The title of this book came from a sermon that I delivered many years ago regarding how to obtain salvation. In a conversation with Nicodemus, the Savior says, "Ye <u>must</u> be born again." Upon further reflection on this theme, however, I have come to the realization that there is an even greater "must" regarding the Christian life—our lives <u>must</u> glorify God.

I am of the opinion that the Body of Christ as a whole can no longer afford to continue living with one foot in the church and one in the world. The time for "Sunday Only" Christianity has gone. Becoming a Christian is not an event that begins and ends with the prayer of salvation. Being a Christian is a daily, life-long process of being transformed from glory to glory into His image (II Corinthians 3:18). This process begins with salvation and is continually "walked out" in our daily lives by allowing the Spirit of God to gradually renew our minds and thereby change our actions and choices to conform to the standard of Christ.

As we grow in grace and in the knowledge of Jesus Christ and yield our will to the will of God, our very lives bring glory to God. God is glorified when we receive salvation through His Son. God is glorified when we rely on His Word as the standard for our lives. Our lives bring glory to God when we pray in faith. God is glorified when we overcome adversity by applying godly principles. God is also glorified when we praise and thank Him for His goodness and mercy toward us.

This book is a collection of messages that I have compiled that reflect the ways in which we honor and glorify God. It is my prayer that you will gain a greater understanding of what a true commitment to Christ really entails and a deeper appreciation of the importance of living a Christ-centered life.

Part One:

The *Must* of Salvation

Introduction

Scripture leaves no room for error or misinterpretation concerning the matter of salvation. The Word of God is very clear concerning our need for a Savior. Romans 5:19 states, "For as by one man's disobedience many were made sinners, so by the obedience of one shall many be made righteous." Adam's sin resulted in separation between God and man. Jesus came to reconcile mankind back to God.

Salvation is the gift of God granted only to those who believe on the name of the Lord Jesus Christ (Ephesians 2:8). Salvation cannot be bought or earned. Good works will not get us into Heaven. Church service is insufficient to secure eternal life.

Once we receive the gift of salvation, our names are written in the Lamb's Book of Life and our eternal future is secure. What a blessed assurance! We are members of the royal family of believers with God as our Father and Christ as our elder brother. I John 3:2 captures it so well:

"Beloved, now are we the sons of God, and it doth not yet appear what we shall be: but we know that, when He shall appear, we shall be like Him; for we shall see Him as he is."

THE MUST OF THE MATTER

"There was a man of the Pharisees, named Nicodemus, a ruler of the Jews: The same came to Jesus by night, and said unto him, Rabbi, we know that thou art a teacher come from God: for no man can do these miracles that thou doest, except God be with him. Jesus answered and said unto him, Verily, verily, I say unto thee, Except a man be born again, he cannot see the kingdom of God. Nicodemus saith unto him, How can a man be born when he is old? Can he enter the second time into his mother's womb, and be born? Jesus answered, Verily, verily, I say unto thee, Except a man be born of water and of the Spirit, he cannot enter into the kingdom of God. That which is born of the flesh is flesh; and that which is born of the Spirit is spirit. Marvel not that I said unto thee, Ye must be born again."

John 3:1-7

The nighttime encounter between Jesus and Nicodemus is a very familiar story. It has been preached across the length and breadth of this nation and around the globe for many years. This account has also been the focus of countless Sunday School lessons. I personally have delivered many sermons from many different platforms concerning this story. However, one morning during my personal study time, the Holy Spirit focused my attention on a single word in that seventh verse—MUST. When I came to the word *must*, it took on a neon-like radiance and seemed to flash on the page before my eyes. It commanded my attention and, the more I tried to read on, the more I was captivated by this one word—*Must*.

Must brings a sense of urgency and seriousness to any matter. When we find ourselves having to respond to a situation where a *must* is involved, we are stripped of all other alternatives. This simple four-letter word in the book of Saint John Chapter 3, impacts the seventh verse in its entirety. When it comes to salvation, there's a *must* to that matter. When it comes to seeing God's face in peace, there is a *must* to that matter. We won't get into Heaven by accident or by coincidence. Those of us who make it in will have paid proper respect to the *must* of the matter. If you're not attentive to the *must*, you'll end up losing your soul.

> **If you're not attentive to the *must*, you'll end up losing your soul.**

The Must of the Matter

Jesus was in a certain city when He received a nighttime visitor. Permit me to say a few words about this visitor. I will likewise say a few words about the One who was visited. The visitor was named Nicodemus. The first thing that Scripture informs us of regarding this man is that he came seeking Jesus at night. No matter the time of day, it's always good for men to seek Jesus. A group of men saw a star in the east around the time of our Savior's birth and they came to Bethlehem seeking Jesus. These seekers are commonly referred to as wise men.

I submit to you that wise men still seek Him. I have noticed that a rather disturbing notion exists within the Body of Christ—the notion that Christianity is mainly for women. In many households, the wives attend church while the husbands stay home. God never intended for it to be that way. While it is true that in many of our churches women outnumber men as much as ten to one; our families and communities will never be all that God intends for them to be, until the men seek Jesus.

It's a wonderful thing when a man seeks the Lord. Every wife needs a husband who seeks the Lord. Every child needs a father who seeks the Lord. A man who seeks the Lord makes a better husband. A man who truly seeks the Lord makes a better father.

Our Lord promises that if we seek Him, we shall find Him (Luke 11:9). Nicodemus sought the Master and found Him. I think I ought to tell you that Nicodemus wasn't officially on Jesus' agenda. Nicodemus didn't get in touch with Him earlier; still Jesus knew he was coming. Jesus was already in the house waiting for him.

When Jesus was in a village called Sychar, He sat at Jacob's well waiting for the Samaritan woman (John 4:5-29). He knew that she would show up. He knows that someone is seeking Him now and the Lord is poised, ready, and waiting to receive all who seek Him.

Permit me to say a little more about this visitor. Nicodemus was no vagabond Jew. The text reveals that he was a ruler of the Jews. Nicodemus was a member of a very prestigious crowd—The Sanhedrin Council. The Sanhedrin Council was the Supreme Court of Judaism. Nicodemus was also a man of great wealth. Everybody who was anybody in Judaism knew Nicodemus. Nicodemus was *somebody*, and this *somebody* came to see Jesus.

Despite Nicodemus' station in life, Jesus was the heavyweight in that meeting. I often tell people not to come to church and get their heavyweights mixed up. No matter how well he prays, the deacon is not the heavyweight in the church. Now matter how well a choir member may sing, he or she is not the heavyweight in the church. The heavyweight in the church is not the trustee or even the pastor. The ultimate heavyweight in the church is Jesus! You can always tell when people have their heavyweights mixed up. They start strutting around the church—styling and profiling. They think of themselves more highly than they ought. They associate only with people who have certain titles or degrees. They only want to get to know the doctors, lawyers and other "successful" members of the church. They don't have time for the church mother on a fixed income or the single mother on public assistance. They have their heavyweights mixed up!

The first time I saw the movie, *Gone with the Wind*, I noticed that they scrolled a list of credits at the beginning of the movie. I saw the name CLARK GABEL in large print. Then I saw the name of the woman who played Scarlett, VIVIAN LEE, in large print. They co-starred in the movie. They shared equal billing. They were of equal prominence. I am sorry to report that there are some people in the church who want to co-star with Jesus. They want to eclipse the Lord in prominence and prestige, but they can't co-star with the bright and morning star! He's in a class all by Himself.

So Nicodemus was a man of great prominence who was also very religious. How do we know he was religious? Nicodemus was a Pharisee. The Pharisees were a religious group who prided themselves on their outward acts of religious service.

Nicodemus was even a good man. Now you may be thinking, "Well preacher, you've already said he was religious. Wouldn't that automatically make him good?" Not necessarily. It's possible for a person to be very religious without being good. It's possible for a person to be caught up in religious ceremonialism and ritualism and still be no good. I know some church folk who are very religious. They know where "Amen" goes. They know the appropriate time and place to say, "Hallelujah" and "Praise the Lord." They know that the communion table is for the sacraments. They know that you are not to place anything on the communion table that's not sacred. They know that you eat the bread first and you drink the wine second, but being outwardly religious does not necessarily make one good.

Let me refresh your memory. There were some religious folk in Jerusalem—chief priests, scribes, and Pharisees—who concocted a plan to kill Jesus (Matthew 26:3-4). These were church folk and you couldn't beat them being religious. Jesus said that there will be a crowd that will come in the latter day saying, "Lord, have we not prophesied in thy name and in thy name have cast out devils and in thy name done many wonderful works?" Jesus will say to them, "I never knew you: depart from me, ye that work iniquity" (Matthew 7:22-23). Do you know that it's possible to go straight to Hell right through the doors of the church?

> **Do you know that it's possible to go straight to Hell right through the doors of the church?**

Nicodemus began the conversation with such lofty compliments. He said, "Rabbi, we know that thou art a teacher come from God: for no man can do these miracles that thou doest, except God be with Him" (John 3:2). That was nice, but that fell far short of giving Jesus proper recognition. It didn't even begin to describe Jesus' true identity. If you would allow me to paraphrase, Nicodemus told him, "Jesus, we've been watching you. We've admired you and have been fascinated by your ministry. Now I know that there are some Pharisees who are against you, but not all of us are against you. Some of us have been admiring you from a distance. We've had your ministry under close scrutiny. We know about the miracles that you have performed. We know that you stopped through Cana of Galilee and changed water into wine (John 2:1-11). We know about the various times that you suspended the laws of nature and science and worked miracles. We know that you are a teacher come from God. For nobody can do the miracles that you are doing except God be with him. God is with you! He's with you!"

Nicodemus used such flattery. All you have to do to win some folk over is flatter them. If you just butter them up, you've got them. When I was a child my grandmother taught me that nobody goes through the trouble of putting butter on a biscuit unless they're getting ready to put the bite to it!

Flattery didn't get Nicodemus to first base with Jesus. Jesus didn't stop to say, "Well, thank you! That's very kind of you." He bypassed all of that and went straight to the nitty-gritty. Jesus said, "Verily, verily, (which is to say, "Truly, truly") I say unto thee, except a man be born again, he cannot see the kingdom of God," (John 3:3). Nicodemus responded, "Now wait a minute, this dialogue has taken an unexpected turn. Born again? What are you talking about? Are you suggesting that I go back a second time into my mother's womb and be reborn? How can a man be born when he's old?" (John 3:4).

Nicodemus was operating in the physical, but Jesus was operating in the spiritual. Nicodemus needed to raise his level of consciousness. Jesus was not speaking of a physical birth; He was referring to a spiritual birth. It would have been ludicrous for Jesus to suggest that we go back into our mothers' wombs and be reborn. We've already done that once and it wasn't enough. We were all born that way once and it didn't save us! Why would Jesus suggest that we do it all over again?

Jesus was speaking of a different birth. He was talking about being born of the Spirit. He said, "That which is born of the flesh is flesh; and that which is born of the Spirit is spirit. Marvel not that I said unto thee, ye must be born again," (John 3:6-7). Being born again is a <u>must</u>, and if we would enter heaven, we must attend to the must of the matter.

Salvation is a gift of God that is not based on our good works (Ephesians 2:8-9). There is nothing that we can do to deserve it or earn it. As wonderful as it is to visit the sick, that won't get you in. You can get in your car and visit the sick everyday, but if you fail to deal with the must of the matter, you're going to Hell. Before getting on the usher board, make sure you address the must of the matter. Don't even think about putting on a choir robe before you spend time on the must of the matter. I think I ought to tell you that you can't sing your way to Heaven. In fact, you might not have a voice at all but if you deal with the must of the matter, you are saved. You may not be able to quote Scripture, but if you attend to the must of the matter you are in the family!

You might genuinely be a good person. You might have a good heart, but you still must be born again. You can't make it into Heaven with just a good heart. If being good-hearted were all that it took, Jesus wouldn't have had to come. Some people were just born with good hearts. Some of us are better by nature than others are by practice. Some folk will give you the shirts off their backs, but they still have to mind the must of the matter.

What is this mysterious thing called being born again? What is the new birth? The new birth is a spiritual transformation that occurs when one receives Jesus the Christ. Scripture says that if we will confess that Jesus is Lord and believe in our hearts that God raised Him from the dead, we will be saved (Romans 10:9). Your facial features remain the same. The texture of your hair stays the same. Your fingerprints remain the same. All of your physical features go unchanged, but something tremendous takes place on the inside. This change occurs when Jesus takes up residence within you. You die to self and become a new creature in Christ Jesus (II Corinthians 5:17).

Being born again is not being *whitewashed*. Being born again is being *washed white*. When something is whitewashed, you slap a coat of paint on it but the scars and disfigurements are still under the paint. But when you've been washed white, you've been transformed. Filth that's on the inside is washed out. Our sins are forgiven and no longer held against us.

Something happens in the mind of a person who is born again. When you've been born again, you can't hate the folk that you used to despise. You can do good to those who spitefully use you. You can pray for your enemies and bless those that curse you.

When you've been born again, God gives you joy for your sorrow, gladness for your sadness, strength for your weakness and light for your darkness. When you've been born again, you become a citizen of a new city. You have some real estate in a new realm.

I sometimes think about the things that I don't have down here, then the Holy Spirit reminds me of what I will have over there. Over there, we will have eternal rest and peace. All sickness and suffering will be over. All of the trials and tribulations of this life will be over and we will be with the Lord forever. What a wonderful time it will be!

When you've been born again, you become a joint heir with Christ (Romans 8:15-17). You can walk like you're rich when you don't have a dime in the bank. When you're born again you can hold your head up and know that, if your father and your mother forsake you, the Lord will take you up (Psalms 27:10). When you're born again, you've got strength that you never had before. But in order to have that assurance, you have to address the *must* of the matter.

THE MIDDLE MAN

> "And there were also two other, malefactors, led with him to be put to death. And when they were come to the place which is called Calvary, there they crucified him, and the malefactors, one on the right hand, and another on the left."
>
> *Luke 23:32-33*

The scene recorded in this portion of Scripture is not a festive occasion. The hour is not one of joy and happiness. The hour is sad, dark and filled with despair. Three men are being put to death on a hill called Calvary. The hearts of some are locked in an inescapable fear. Some have run away and, at this very hour, are hiding themselves, because it is dangerous to be associated with Jesus. Three men now hang on three crosses positioned side-by-side on the hill. This message, however, will neither focus on the fellow hanging on the left nor the one who hangs on the right. We will instead focus our attention on the man who hangs in the middle. Jesus is "The Middle Man."

A series of events have already taken place prior to our text. Our Lord has already had His praying ground intruded upon by soldiers who came to take Him away. Jesus received a kiss of betrayal from one of His own followers. Judas Iscariot, Jesus' own disciple, delivered our Lord over to His enemies for thirty pieces of silver. Judas kissed Jesus but that kiss was not one of affection but was actually a signal identifying Jesus as the one who was to be taken away (Mark 14:43-45).

Jesus has already been to the hall of the high priest, Caiaphas, and been interrogated (Matthew 26:57-66). The record tells us that because the Jewish kingdom was under Roman rule, they could not pronounce the death sentence (John 18:31). In order to legally take Jesus' life, it was necessary that a Roman official pronounce the death sentence. So they marched our Savior from the hall of the priest to the hall of the governor.

The governor, Pontius Pilate, did not want to get involved in this local religious matter, so he immediately sent Jesus away to the hall of the Jewish king, Herrod. Herrod sent him right back to the hall of Pontius Pilate. The record tells us that Pilate was then forced to decide what to do concerning this man called Jesus. Pilate's wife had a worrisome dream concerning Jesus and she told him to have nothing to do with that just man (Matthew 27:19). Unfortunately, Pilate was a crowd-pleaser. He did whatever it took to keep the crowd happy. So, to satisfy the rowdy and unruly crowd, Pilate decided to comply with their wishes (Mark 15:15). The record tells us that after Pilate had

Jesus beaten, our Savior, Jesus the Christ, was sent forth to be crucified at the outskirts of town.

Our Savior's hands were nailed to the cross. I hate that they bothered His hands. I wish they had left His hands alone for His hands weren't ordinary hands. Jesus' hands were sacred hands. His hands were miracle-working hands. They should have left His hands alone! On one occasion those hands restored sight to the eyes of a blind man (John 9:1-7). Those same hands once held two fish and five loaves of bread and miraculously fed five thousand (John 6:1-11). I wish they had left His hands alone!

They also nailed His feet. I'm so sorry that they bothered His feet. Those feet were unusual feet. In the fourth watch of the night, those feet walked on the water (Matthew 14:25). How I wish those feet had been left alone, but they were nailed to the cross.

Which brings us to our text. Our Lord hangs from a cross on Calvary. That's where our Master is in this portion of Scripture. Don't look for Him any longer in Cana of Galilee. He has already been there. He has already saved the day at a wedding feast by changing water to wine (John 2:1-11). Don't look for Him in the home of Mary, Martha and Lazarus in Bethany for He is not there. He had been there on several occasions and on one occasion He raised Lazarus from the dead (John 11:38-44). At this time, if you want to find Jesus, you have to go to the hill called Calvary.

It is necessary that every child of God periodically return to Calvary to remember the price that was paid to redeem our souls from eternal death. I believe that the reason why some have grown cold in their walk with the Master is that they have stayed away from the hill too long.

It is necessary that every child of God periodically return to Calvary to remember the price that was paid to redeem our souls from eternal death.

Jesus is on the hill now, but He is not alone. There are two other men being executed on the same hill. Two thieves are being put to death on either side of Jesus. It's a dark hour. It's an hour filled with pain and agony. At this time it seems like God Himself has turned His back on Jesus. Peering through this veil of sorrow and agony, however, I see a sense of order on Calvary.

With the crosses strategically arranged on Calvary, I tell you there is order on the hill. The crosses were placed side by side and there is not one cross out of place. The soldiers didn't know what they were doing, but they have lined up everything just as it ought to be on the hill. Isn't it strange how the Lord works things out? Sometimes our Lord can use our enemies to put things in perfect order.

A close examination of this scene shows that there is a problem on the right hand and a problem on the left hand but the solution to every problem hangs in the middle. Jesus is the Middle Man! I submit to you that Jesus' position between the two men

The Middle Man

mirrors His divine position between man and man. I have come to discover that one person will never be what he should be toward another person without the aid of the Middle Man. It takes the Middle Man to keep us in touch with one another. So many friendships are quickly dissolved because the parties involved have tried to transact the business of friendship without the Middle Man. If you are having problems in your relationships with friends or family members, call on the Middle Man. If you are having problems in your marriage, bring the Middle Man into your relationship! Husbands, you can trust the Middle Man with you wives. Our Lord specializes in healing relationships.

Jesus is also suspended between earth and heaven indicating that He also acts as the Middle Man between man and God. Jesus came to earth to redeem mankind from their sins. As our Lord hung there suspended between two men and between earth and heaven, He was ridiculed and taunted by His enemies. As His enemies were marching around the cross—dancing and mocking—Jesus looked down upon them and said, "Father, forgive them; for they know not what they do" (Luke 23:34-37).

In business transactions, it's been said that in order to earn greater profits, you have to cut out the middle man. That may work in the business arena, but it does not work in the business of redemption. If we would transact the business of salvation, it must be done through the Middle Man. How do I know this? Jesus told us this on one occasion when He said, "I am the way, the truth, and the life: no man cometh unto the Father, but by me," (John 14:6). No man can bypass Jesus. The song says, "Soon and very soon we are going to see the King," but not before we have first done business with the Middle Man.

The record tells us that Jesus died. He said, "Father, into thy hand I commend my spirit," (Luke 23:46). They took His body down from the cross and carried Him to the tomb of a man called Joseph of Arimathea. They buried the Lord's body in a borrowed tomb (Luke 23:50-53).

When I was a child, I wondered why Jesus' burial place was referred to as a "borrowed tomb." As I grew older, I came to understand that you have no plans of keeping anything that is borrowed. When you borrow something, you intend to use it for a while and then return it to the owner. Jesus knew that He would rise again and had, in fact, told His disciples of His resurrection (Mark 8:31). Since Jesus did not remain in the tomb, it was only borrowed.

> **Jesus is our Middle Man because He took our place and died for our sins.**

Jesus is our Middle Man because He took our place and died for our sins. He died a substitutionary death there on Calvary, so that we might have life and have it more abundantly. The reason I am here today is because the Lord brought me; He is the MIDDLE MAN. He is the reason I sing, "At the Cross, at the Cross", but the cross would have no relevance if it were not for the Middle Man.

STORIES OF THE LOST AND FOUND

"What man of you, having an hundred sheep, if he lose one of them, doth not leave the ninety and nine in the wilderness, and go after that which is lost, until he find it? And when he hath found it, he layeth it on his shoulders, rejoicing. And when he cometh home, he calleth together his friends and neighbours, saying unto them, Rejoice with me; for I have found my sheep which was lost. I say unto you, that likewise joy shall be in heaven over one sinner that repenteth, more than over ninety and nine just persons, which need no repentance. Either what woman having ten pieces of silver, if she lose one piece, doth not light a candle, and sweep the house, and seek diligently till she find it? And he said, A certain man had two sons: And the younger of them said to his father, Father, give me the portion of goods that falleth to me. And he divided unto them his living."

Luke 15:4-8 & 11-12

Jesus spoke these parables to a group who was highly critical of His messianic ministry. The Pharisees focused their efforts on the mere appearance of righteousness. Their prayers and charitable acts were done to impress men rather than to please God. The Pharisees were disturbed with Jesus because He exposed their hypocrisy. Jesus taught His disciples not to engage in righteous acts just to be seen of men.

Jesus instructed His disciples not to make a public spectacle of giving to the needy as the hypocrites did. He said that acts of charity should be done in secret (Matthew 6:4). He also exposed the fact that the hypocrite took pride in praying long drawn out prayers on the street corners just to be seen of men. He told His disciples, "When you pray enter into your closet, pray in secret, and God will reward you openly," (Matthew 6:6). Scripture says that if you do good deeds in order to obtain the praise of others, this alone will be your reward.

The objective of our work should be to glorify God rather than seeking self-glory. If your objective is to seek the spotlight, you will have no reward in the Kingdom of God (Matthew 6:1). The Lord promises that if we would first seek the Kingdom of God and its righteousness then all of these other things will be added (Matthew 6:33). As a result of His teachings, the Pharisees became arch opponents and enemies of Jesus. They conspired, plotted and planned that they might be rid of Jesus the Christ.

I've come to discover that there are some things we're going to have to endure on this Christian journey. If you have decided to make Jesus your choice, you can expect some opposition. If you have been mistreated or wounded by someone who has sought to do you in, think about who walked the path ahead of you. Jesus had done no wrong, but was a victim of hostility and evil treatment.

There was some concern on the part of the religious community because Jesus spent time with sinners. Scripture says that the Pharisees and scribes murmured because He received sinners and ate with them (Luke 15:1-2). So, in our text, the Savior addresses a group of murmuring, critical folk. You know the kind. They are quick to be sarcastic and slow to sing praises. They only see what's wrong with you and never see anything right.

> **If you have decided to make Jesus your choice, you can expect some opposition.**

Jesus' response came in the form of three parables. Each parable revolved around something or someone that was lost. I'm happy to report that, in each of these stories, that which was lost was later found.

In many local department stores, grocery stores and other public places, there is what is commonly referred to as the "Lost and Found Department." These various places have such a department because, if someone should lose a personal item while there, they have a place to go to retrieve what was lost. All of humanity can be viewed as such—consisting of souls that are either lost or found. In spite of all of the many efforts on the part of the church to win souls, there are still many souls that are lost. This world also consists of souls that, like the song, "*Amazing Grace*" describes were once lost but now are found; blind but now can see.

Let's delve into the "*Stories of the Lost and Found*":

The Parable of the Lost Sheep

In this parable, a shepherd originally had one hundred sheep but is now left with ninety-nine. The loss of one sheep has changed the total. Losing one has made a difference. If you wish to purchase an item that costs exactly one hundred dollars, ninety-nine dollars won't do. Thus, one becomes very important.

Scripture says that the shepherd went to great lengths—even to the point of going out into the wilderness—to look for that one lost sheep. The sheep was lost and the shepherd left the ninety-nine to search for the one that was lost in the wilderness.

I'm happy to report that his search was successful. He found that lost sheep. I thank God that someone went out and found me. In fact, neither you nor I would be in church today had someone not gone out and found us. Someone cared enough about us to journey into the wilderness of our torn and shattered lives to find us.

Christians must have deep concern for the lost. We must seek to find those who are lost. Jesus commands His disciples, "Go ye therefore, and teach all nations…" (Matthew 28:19). God has issued us a commandment that takes us beyond the walls of the church. We come to church to be equipped and to sharpen our tools, but we must go out into the world and find the lost. The church must be more than a football field where we gather in huddles and pass the ball from one Christian to another and never seek those who are lost. We have to be about the business of beckoning lost souls.

The Church's purpose is not to build great buildings. Great facilities have their merit, but the purpose of the Church is to build people. We must neither be deterred nor sidetracked from our purpose in the world. We've been chosen. God has saved us so that we might help lead others to the saving grace of Jesus Christ.

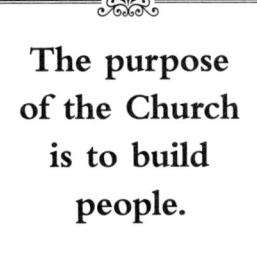

The purpose of the Church is to build people.

The Parable of the Lost Coin

Jesus carried it a little farther in the second parable by talking not about a lost sheep but about a lost coin. He speaks of a woman who had ten pieces of silver and one piece was lost. The record says the woman put forth a great effort to find that lost coin by lighting her lamps and sweeping her floors. When we share Jesus with others, that's all we're doing—sweeping. Every child of God ought to go about during the course of the day sweeping for lost souls. You may not recover a lost soul every time, but, if you are persistent in your sweeping, your persistence will pay off. She found that lost piece of silver and the record says that she called her friends and neighbors, and said, "Rejoice with me; for I have found the piece which I had lost" (Luke 15:9).

The Prodigal Son

Now, the last of the three stories is neither that of a lost sheep nor that of a lost coin, but that of a lost soul, the "Prodigal Son." The record tells us that this young man approached his father and said, "Father, give me the portion of goods that falleth to me," (Luke 15:12). The father agreed and the son took his inheritance and went to a far country. He wanted to put some distance between him and his father. He wanted to be out of his father's sight because he wanted to engage in activity that his father would not have approved of. It's important to establish godly standards at home. Children should learn that some activities and forms of entertainment are not allowed in their parents' home and parents should set that standard.

The young man took his inheritance and went to a far country. The record tells us, however, that his circumstances changed. He entered that country rich but one morning found himself extremely poor. Scripture tells us that he "wasted his substance with riotous living," (Luke 15:13). He wasted all that his father had worked so hard to give him—what a shame. The late Dr.

C.L. Franklin made an observation on this very subject. He said that want always follows waste. If you waste your money, one day you'll want it. If you waste or abuse your influence, one day you'll wish you had it. If you waste your health, one day you'll want it. For in every instance, want always follows waste.

The young man wasted what the father had given him. We must not come down too hard on this young man because, if you think about it, each of us have been guilty of wasting what was given to us by our Father. We have all wasted our money, talent and, most of all, time on things that were of little or no benefit to anyone and brought no glory to God.

After a period of splurging and sinful wasting, the record says that he awakened to discover that he was in want. The son received a rude awakening; no man gave to him. None of his friends who had received from him would help him in his time of need. I say frequently that it's bad enough to be broke at home, but it's worse when you're broke in a far country. If you're broke at home, maybe someone who knew your grandmother or somebody who was a good friend of your mother or a good friend of your father will have compassion on you. When you're broke in a far country, however, nobody knows you or your family and that's far worse.

The record tells us that he began to be in want. But something else happened to compound that problem. A mighty famine arose in that land. When a famine arises and the economy is affected, people aren't as benevolent as they otherwise would be. In a time of economic crisis even well-meaning people aren't as generous. When they see the man outside the mall collecting donations for the Salvation Army, they aren't as quick to drop something in the kettle when times are hard. They tend to keep close scrutiny on their bank accounts because there is a famine in the land.

So, a mighty famine arose in that land and the boy began to be in want. According to the Scripture, he sought employment. He thought he could acquire a prestigious position. I'm sure he thought to himself, "Surely I will find a job worthy of my station in life." But the only employment he could find was working for a member of the Gentile community. In his time of need and want, his own Jewish friends did not aid him. He could only get help from a Gentile. The record tells us that the Gentile gave him a menial job feeding swine.

If you want to see how the mighty have fallen, come with me to the hog pen. Let's journey now. It's feeding time. This young man's bad choices have now brought him down to the level of a hog pen. He is now the caretaker of swine. What a menial job. Look at him. His once royal robe is now ragged. As he makes his way to the hog pen, the princely sandals that once adorned his feet are now ragged, worn and thin. He makes his way to the hog pen in a ragged robe and worn sandals. Look at him.

I know the record tells us the circumstances, but since I'm a country boy, let me tell it like this. He's on his way to the hog pen with the slop bucket in his hands. Look at him. I can see a little slop from the bucket splatter on his robe and even on his face. He pauses, sets the bucket down for a moment and wipes the slop from his face. He pauses for a moment and brushes the filth from his robe that by now is covered with pig grime. His once regal garments now carry the stench of the hog pen.

I also imagine that the hogs have now caught the scent of the slop. I can see them galloping to the trough and to the fence. I can see them as he pours the slop into the trough. I can see them rooting each other to get their heads down to where the is.

Scripture tells us that the young son just watched the swine eat. The boy just sat there no doubt with his hand under his chin just watching the hogs. While he was sitting there hungry, he desired to eat what the hogs ate. In my boyhood they used to sing a song, *"If I'm too high Lord please bring me down."* I want to serve notice that this is a request that you don't have to make. Just stay up there with your head in the clouds. Keep feeling yourself better than everybody else and I declare the Lord in His own time will bring you down!

While he was in that hog pen, he thought about his father's house. It's sad but true that sometimes it takes hitting rock bottom to bring some of us to our senses. Some of us have to fall down before we'll look up. Sometimes it takes bad things happening to us to bring us to the realization that all that we need can be found in our Father's house.

While sitting there, he thinks about his father's house and the Bible says he came to himself. He says to himself, "How many hired servants of my father's have bread enough and to spare, and I perish with hunger!" (Luke 15:17). The servants don't own anything, yet they lack nothing. They don't own anything, but they have bread enough and some to spare. Here he is, a rich man's son, and he is about to perish with hunger. I can hear him say, "Now, I'm in the hog pen and I'm in the mud, but I don't have to stay here. I know where I am, but I don't have to remain at this location. I know what I'll do. I'm going to rise and go back to my father's house. I'm going to rise and go back to the man that I never should have left. I'm going to confess all that I have done. I'm not going to *ease* in acting like I've never done anything wrong. I'm going to make a sincere confession."

Scripture says that he was on his way home, and when he got fairly close, the father who was standing in the doorway ran out to meet his son. The father was looking for him. I know he was looking because he would not have seen him coming had he not been looking.

I want to tell you that our Heavenly Father is looking right now. Once you start back home, you'll find that you won't even have to knock! You'll find that you won't even have to ring the doorbell! He's already looking for you!

Well, the father saw him coming and, when he realized that the figure in the distance was his child, he ran to meet him. You should have been there to see that father running to meet his child—running with outstretched arms, running with a smile on his face, running to meet his son. He wrapped his arms around him and kissed him. He expressed his love and affection for his son.

In essence, the son said, "Wait Daddy before you get too happy. I could lie and say that I was robbed of everything that I had. But I'm coming back to tell you the truth of the matter. Father, I have sinned against heaven, and before thee and am no more worthy to be called thy son: make me as one of thy hired servants" (Luke 15:18-19). Notice that his words have changed from "give me" to "make me". The lyrics changed from "give me" to "make me". I submit to you that this was the correct posture to take. Our prayers ought to have fewer "give me[s]" and more "make me[s]".

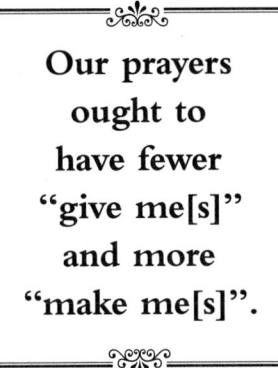

> **Our prayers ought to have fewer "give me[s]" and more "make me[s]".**

Well, the father didn't scorn or ridicule him. The father didn't rebuke him. Instead, the father said to his servants, "Come here servants. Go and get my best robe and put it on him. Go and get a ring and put it on his finger. Go get shoes and put them on his feet and go and kill the fatted calf. Make a feast and call all of my friends and neighbors. Tell them to come and rejoice with me for my son that was dead is now alive. My son who was lost is now found," (Luke 15:22-24).

In this series of stories, Jesus teaches an important lesson. In each story that which was lost was eventually found. So it sends a message to all of us that all lost things have the potential for being found. Now, our individual stories began with us being lost. All of our stories began with us being lost because we were born in sin and shaped in iniquity (Psalm 51:5). But I'm glad to tell you that your story does not have to end with your being lost. The record tells us that in each case all that were lost were later found. That's a good way for a man's story to end. Don't let your story end with your being lost, but let your story end with your being found. The Prodigal Son had his story, but I have my story. My story started with my being lost, but I rejoice in telling you that it won't end that way. Like the lost sheep, the lost coin and the lost son, I was lost, but the good news is, now I am found.

DON'T TURN THIS INVITATION DOWN

> "And Moses said unto Hobab, the son of Raguel the Midianite, Moses' father in law, We are journeying unto the place of which the Lord said, I will give it you: come thou with us, and we will do thee good: for the Lord hath spoken good concerning Israel."
>
> *Numbers 10:29*

What an awesome invitation! It is an invitation that comes from Moses to his father-in-law, Hobab. As he was leading the Children of Israel to the Promised Land, Moses seemed to say, "If you'll come with us, you won't regret it. If you'll come with us, you'll be happy that you did because where we're going will be so much better than where we've been. Come with us because we're going to a place where the land flows with milk and honey." I submit to you that the invitation that Moses extends to Hobab, in a manner of speaking, is an invitation still extended to us today. We still have before us the opportunity to go to a heavenly Promised Land.

I wish I could have talked to Hobab on the heels of this invitation, but I arrived on the scene too late. Unfortunately, I was born too late to catch up with Hobab, but thanks be to God that I am able to catch up with you because this is the greatest invitation that you will ever receive. I, therefore, must tell you now (as I would have told Hobab then), **"Don't turn this invitation down."**

Over the course of our lives, we have all received invitations to take advantage of a variety of opportunities. We have been invited to join others in various activities and events. We all have been afforded opportunities to join certain groups and be a part of countless planned activities. I have arrived at the conclusion that, once you have decided to make Jesus your choice, you can't accept every invitation. Some invitations are to engage in activities that are not appropriate for the children of God. We must, therefore, turn some invitations down.

The invitation extended in our text, however, is well worth accepting. To fully realize the importance of this invitation, we should first examine the events and circumstances that have occurred prior to the time of our text. Our text focuses on a people about whom much is recorded in Scripture, the Children of Israel. The record informs us that they have already crossed the Red Sea and witnessed the drowning of Pharaoh's hostile army (Exodus 14). They have sojourned in the wilderness of Shur and camped by the pools of Marah. They have also witnessed the bitter waters of Marah become sweet (Exodus 15:22-25). The record tells us that after moving from the pools of Marah, they camped at the foot of Mount Sinai. God summoned Moses to the top of Mount Sinai. During their one-on-one meeting, God gave Moses clear instructions on how to prepare the people to hear directly from Him (Exodus 19:9-13).

God summoned Moses to the top of Mount Sinai and away from the people so that He could speak to Moses alone. There are times when God wants our undivided attention. During these times of solitude, God is able to give divine direction and order to our lives. On the third day, the Children of Israel received a series of laws commonly known as the Ten Commandments (Exodus 20).

> During these times of solitude, God is able to give divine direction and order to our lives.

It is now moving time. God has given marching orders. At the time of our text, the children of Israel have resumed their march to the land of promise. Those of us who make it in must keep on marching. You may stop for a while but you must keep marching. Life circumstances may cause you to stop for a while to regain your strength and composure, but always remember that you must keep marching! Come with me to the camp and witness the unfolding of the events of the text.

Moses extends an invitation to Hobab. He says, "We are journeying unto the place of which the LORD said, I will give it you:

come thou with us, and we will do thee good: for the LORD hath spoken good concerning Israel," (Numbers 10:29). Hobab responds by saying, "I will not go; but I will depart to mine own land, and to my kindred," (Numbers 10:30). Hobab wanted to return to his native land. He wanted to go back to the life that he once had. Moses had a strong desire for Hobab to continue. Moses replied, "Leave us not, I pray thee… if thou go with us, yea, it shall be, that what goodness the LORD shall do unto us, the same will we do unto thee," (Numbers 10:31-32). In other words, Moses indicates that God's promises will extend to Hobab if he will only abandon his thoughts of returning home.

I've come to discover an important similarity between Moses and the children of Israel going to their earthly Promised Land and our going to the heavenly Promised Land sometimes referred to as Beulah Land or Glory Land. In order to gain possession of their Promised Land, the children of Israel had to divorce themselves from the land of Egypt. The problem that many of us have, which hinders our efforts to make it to the heavenly Promised Land, is our unwillingness to cut loose from the sinful "Egypts" of our past. I must warn you here that in order to grab hold of one, you must loose the other.

Scholars suggest that Moses' invitation was extended with such excitement and enthusiasm that it moved Hobab to continue. I think that when you're telling other people about the goodness of God, you ought to have some excitement. When you're trying to persuade other people to join you on your journey, you ought to beam with enthusiasm. You can't sell me on something that you're not excited about! <u>You</u> ought to have some enthusiasm.

Now the record tells us that Moses speaks to him and, through the aid of the Holy Spirit and my spiritual imagination, I entered the camp and listened as the great patriarch, Moses, talked to his father-in-law, Hobab. He tells him, "We are headed to a great land and I wish you would go with us." I overheard Moses telling Hobab, "Now I want you to know whether you go with us or not, we're still going! We're going if we have to go by ourselves. Our hearts are fixed and our minds are made up. I've been up on the mountain. Jehovah has talked with me. Yahweh has communicated with me. El Elyon has dialogued with me and we're headed to the Promised Land. We had a brief stop here at the base of this mountain because God had some business to attend to, but the time has come for us to resume our journey. Come with us. You won't regret it. Come with us and we will do thee good."

Moses also indicates that God's favor was upon Israel. I love to hang out with folk who are enjoying God's favor. I often say that I like to hang with people whose cups are overflowing. I have decided that if I can't be the cup, I'll gladly be the saucer! Don't be envious or jealous when God is blessing somebody else. You better try to get as close to him or her as you can!

The favor of God was upon Moses and the Children of Israel. They had encountered many painful experiences, but now they're on their way to greater things. You may have faced obstacles and hardships, but if you remain faithful, God will bestow His favor upon you. You may be experiencing hostility at the hands of your enemies, but the Holy Spirit would have me to tell you that emancipation is on the way. Don't worry about whose opposing you! Focus on the One who is for you!

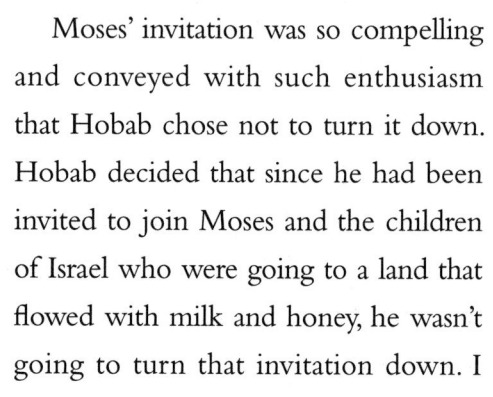

> **Don't worry about whose opposing you! Focus on the One who is for you!**

Moses' invitation was so compelling and conveyed with such enthusiasm that Hobab chose not to turn it down. Hobab decided that since he had been invited to join Moses and the children of Israel who were going to a land that flowed with milk and honey, he wasn't going to turn that invitation down. I think I ought to tell you that Hobab was not an Israelite. Hobab was a Midianite. Hobab wasn't a Jew; he was a Gentile. Despite the difference in nationality and cultural background, Hobab decided that he would not turn Moses' invitation down.

I've been blessed to be invited to some wonderful places. When Mrs. Black and I were invited by President Clinton to have breakfast with him and Hillary at the White House, that was an awesome invitation! When I was invited to go over to Tokyo, Japan to conduct a crusade, that was a great invitation! When I was invited to come to Detroit, Michigan to preach at the New Bethel Baptist Church, that was a great invitation! The late Dr. C. L. Franklin had pastored this historic church for many years. Aretha Franklin's special chauffeur drove us in her personal limousine. That was a great invitation! When I was privileged to preach for the late Dr. E.V. Hill in Los Angeles, California at the Mount Zion Baptist Church, that was a great invitation!

In my life, I've had my share of great invitations. But by far the greatest invitation came from Mother Leona Washington out in the cotton field where I was chopping cotton. She told me, "Jerry you are a good child, but goodness alone won't save you. You've got to be obedient to the plan of salvation." She said, "Jesus died for your sins. There's a revival going on at the West End Baptist Church and, if your parents will grant their permission, I want you to go with me tonight as my guest because Jesus wants to prepare a place for you in the Promised Land." I went home after having finished my work in the field. I was very excited about the revival. Mother Leona Washington was going to carry me personally. Has there been a "Leona Washington" in your life?

I went home and got permission from my mother and grandmother. I took a bath in a number three tin tub and I prepared for the revival. I put on the best clothes that I had and waited on that old mother of the church to carry me to the revival. I sat down on what they called the "mourner's bench." I heard the choir sing. I heard the preacher, Reverend Dr. P.J. Yancey, preach and extend the invitation. Everybody else on the bench got up and left me still sitting there.

Dr. Yancey was preparing to give the benediction when Mother Leona Washington stood up and said, "Brother Pastor, I know it's time for us to go but we got one seeker still left there on the pew and the Lord is speaking to me. I invited him today in the field and the Lord is speaking to me saying we ought to have one more prayer."

I thank God for that one last prayer. She bowed down and started praying with me. She said, "Lord I know you have a way of doing things. Lord I know you have a way of reaching people. Speak to this child. Touch his heart. Move him in the name of Jesus." When the prayer was over, the preacher extended another invitation. That's when the Devil said, "If you get up and go the other folk are going to look at you, your friends are going to laugh at you. If you go, you're going to have to deal with what other folk will say". I thank God that the Holy Spirit told me, "Don't turn this invitation down." I got up from that pew and ran to the front. I gave the preacher my hand and I gave God my heart and I've been running for Him ever since.

An old song of the church extends the following invitation:

"*I heard the voice of Jesus say, 'Come unto me and rest.*
Lay down thou weary one lay down thy head upon My breast.'"

I thank God for the invitation, but once you heed the call and accept the invitation, your lyrics change to:

"*I came to Jesus just as I was. Weary, worn and sad.*
I found in Him a resting place and He has made me glad."

A tremendous privilege is awaiting you. Opportunity is calling you. It's mighty nice to be a child of the King. It's mighty nice to know that if you don't wake up in the morning, everything is all right. The Master is calling you. Please don't turn this invitation down.

Part Two:

THE *MUST* OF PRAYER AND FAITH

Introduction

I was first exposed to the word "faith" in my childhood long before I really knew how important faith was, and still is, in the life of the believer. The dictionary defines the word faith as, "confident belief in the truth, value, or trustworthiness of a person, idea, or thing." I agree with this definition because, where there is true faith, there's confidence. In Christian circles, however, the best-known definition of faith doesn't come from the dictionary but from the Word of God. In Hebrews 11:1, the writer describes faith as, "…the substance of things hoped for, the evidence of things not seen." Faith believes without seeing. When our breakthrough appears impossible, our faith is the evidence (or proof) that it will come to pass. This eleventh chapter of Hebrews also informs us that we must have faith in order to please God (Hebrews 11:6). This verse goes on to say, "…for he that cometh to God must believe that He is, and that he is a rewarder of them that diligently seek Him," indicating the importance of faith in establishing a connection with God.

Prayer is the means by which we establish this connection. Prayer gives us access to the power of God. Through prayer, we bring God's supernatural power into our natural circumstances. In this sixth verse, the writer of Hebrews suggests that effective prayer consists of two key elements: faith in the sovereignty of

God ("that He is") and the faith that earnestly seeking Him will not go unrewarded ("that He is the rewarder of them that diligently seek him."). Scripture says that we walk by faith (II Corinthians 5:7) and we live by faith (Hebrews 10:38). In fact, every act of obedience to the will of God is done by faith.

Both the Old and New Testament provide portraits of faith and prayer that, even today, serve as valuable lessons for believers. The book of Daniel reports on four men of great faith—Shadrach, Meshach, Abednego and Daniel. These four friends found themselves in a strange land surrounded by a Godless people. Yet, despite tremendous pressure to turn from God, these men of faith held fast to their belief in the sovereignty of Jehovah God. As a result, God delivered them from danger.

New Testament accounts of individuals with great faith in the miracle-working power of God are also great sources of encouragement to believers. On numerous occasions, both Jews and Gentiles came to Jesus seeking miracles and the outcomes of their situations were based on their prayers and levels of faith.

Scripture says, "[God] is able to do exceeding abundantly above all that we ask or think, according to the power that worketh in us," (Ephesians 3:20). This power is at work in us by faith, thus it is rightly declared, "Prayer is the key to the Kingdom, but faith unlocks the door."

MIRACLES

"He answered and said, Lo, I see four men loose, walking in the midst of the fire, and they have no hurt; and the form of the fourth is like the Son of God. Then Nebuchadnezzar came near to the mouth of the burning fiery furnace, and spake, and said, Shadrach, Meshach, and Abednego, ye servants of the most high God, come forth, and come hither. Then Shadrach, Meshach, and Abednego, came forth of the midst of the fire. And the princes, governors, and captains, and the king's counsellors, being gathered together, saw these men, upon whose bodies the fire had no power, nor was an hair of their head singed, neither were their coats changed, nor the smell of fire had passed on them."

Daniel 3:25-27

The dictionary defines a miracle as "an extraordinary event manifesting divine intervention in human affairs." In essence, a miracle happens when God takes a quantum leap into our human affairs and suspends the laws of nature. I believe in miracles. I believe in a Higher Power and the ability of that Power to intervene in our circumstances and work miracles. I am, however, acutely aware of the fact that there are those who scoff at or make light of those of us who believe in miracles. They consider a belief in miracles to be ignorant and even foolish; nevertheless, I believe in miracles. Although I stand in opposition to many of the brilliant minds of our time that believe otherwise, my faith in the miracle-working power of God cannot be shaken.

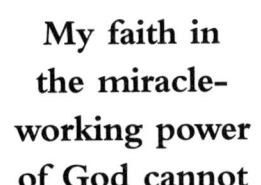

> **My faith in the miracle-working power of God cannot be shaken.**

The Holy Spirit has revealed to me some interesting facts concerning miracles. First, miracles are often preceded by crisis. In other words, crisis often sets the stage for God to work a miracle. Another aspect of miracles is that we can never experience one of God's miracles except we believe in the Miracle Worker. It is imperative that we believe in God as the Miracle Worker. When we believe in the power of God to work miracles in our lives, we are elevated to a higher level of consciousness. Along with a belief in miracles comes the realization that there is no problem that cannot be solved and no sickness that cannot be healed. When we embrace the reality of miracles, we understand there is no bad habit that cannot be broken and no worthwhile goal that cannot be attained.

This third chapter of Daniel records the miraculous story of Shadrach, Meshach and Abednego. These three men were brought before King Nebuchadnezzar because of their failure to bow to a golden image and worship an idol god. The king had promoted these men to positions of prominence and was, therefore, insulted by their refusal to comply with his order. The king summoned the three men to the palace and asked, "Is it true, O Shadrach, Meshach, and Abednego, do not ye serve my gods, nor worship the golden image which I have set up?" (Daniel 3:14) The king reiterated the consequence of failing to bow and brought the power of their God into question. He said, "…[If] ye fall down and worship the image which I have made; [then all is] well: but if ye worship not, ye shall be cast the same hour into the midst of a burning fiery furnace; and who is that God that shall deliver you out of my hands?" (Daniel 3:15)

> We are constantly presented with opportunities to conform to the world's standard or embrace the standard of Christ.

In this day and time, it is rare for the children of God to have their beliefs challenged in such an extreme fashion. In the United States especially, Christians aren't frequently faced with the threat of death for their religious beliefs. Our beliefs are challenged, however, in small ways on a daily basis. In the workplace, in the home and in social settings, we are constantly presented with opportunities to conform to the world's standard or embrace the standard of Christ. For example, in the workplace, do you perform your work as unto the Lord (Ephesians 6:5-7) or do you only do enough to get by? Are you kind to your family members even when no one else is around? How do you treat a store clerk or waiter who has mishandled a transaction? Our religious convictions are challenged in these and many other small ways, and each time we are faced with the unconscious choice to be followers of God or followers of the world.

Shadrach, Meshach, and Abednego responded to the king's threat by saying, "…our God whom we serve is able to deliver us from the burning fiery furnace, and he will deliver us out of thine hand, O king." (Daniel 3:17). In this one statement, these three men expressed their faith in the power of God and their confidence in the fact that God would deliver them from trouble. They went on to say, "But if not, be it known unto thee, O king, that we will not serve thy gods, nor worship the golden image which thou hast set up," (Daniel 3:18). What an odd statement. It seems obvious that, if God didn't deliver them from the furnace, they would not worship other gods. They would all be dead and therefore unable to worship any god. A second look at this statement, however, reveals a profound lesson in faith. Shadrach, Meshach, and Abednego had such faith in the sovereignty of God that, regardless of the outcome of their current situation, no threat of pain or death would diminish their allegiance to the one true God.

The three Hebrews put up no resistance as they were led to the furnace. They marched cooperatively, willingly, and victoriously to the furnace. King Nebuchadnezzar had grown so angry that he commanded that the furnace be heated to seven times its normal temperature (Daniel 3:19). The heat from the furnace was so great that a great blast of fire destroyed the soldiers who threw Shadrach, Meshach, and Abednego into the fire. God will sometimes allow destruction to come to those who place others in harm's way. There is no need for us to worry about those who set traps for us and seek our downfall. We need only remember that if God is for us who can be against us? (Romans 8:31)

As the story of Shadrach, Meshach, and Abednego continues, when the king later looked into the furnace he was so astounded that he could not maintain his royal composure. He called out to his servants who were near and said, "Did not we cast three men bound into the midst of the fire?" (Daniel 3:24) The servants replied, "True, O king." Then the bewildered king said, in essence, "In addition to Shadrach, Meshach, and Abednego, I see a fourth man, a strange looking man. I see a man like no other man I have ever seen before. There is a fourth man in the furnace, and the fourth man looks like the Son of God." The king reversed the sentence and called them out of the furnace. The men emerged from their fiery trial victoriously, without so much as the smell of smoke in their clothing or a hair on their heads singed. God entered Shadrach, Meshach, and Abednego's situation and worked a miracle.

I have often wondered why God would allow this situation to go as far as it did. Why didn't He make it so that their apparent rebellion would just escape the king's attention? Why didn't God change the king's heart and make him more lenient in this situation? Why didn't God deliver the men from the hands of the guards? God could have stepped into this situation much earlier and kept His beloved sons out of the furnace altogether. However, I have learned and Scripture tells us that God sometimes uses trouble to show us something that we would not otherwise be able to see. If the king had not been made aware of their failure to bow, they never would have been brought to trial and their escape from the sentence of death in the fiery furnace would have been credited to chance. If God had simply changed the king's heart, the king would have gotten the credit for delivering the men. If the men had devised an elaborate escape from the hands of the guards, Shadrach, Meshach and Abednego would have been credited with their own deliverance. By allowing this situation to progress to the point that it did, no one but God could get the credit for delivering these men from trouble.

Jesus' earthly ministry provides vivid examples of God's desire to receive glory during times of crisis. In the ninth chapter of the gospel of John, Jesus and His disciples encountered a man who was blind from birth. His disciples thought that his blindness was the result of sin on his part or on the part of one or both of his parents. Jesus said, "Neither hath this man sinned, nor his parents: but that the works of God should be made manifest in him," (John 9:3). Jesus healed the man and the man went on to tell his neighbors about Jesus.

Another familiar example revolves around the death of Lazarus. When Jesus was told of Lazarus' illness, He said, "This sickness is not unto death, but for the glory of God, that the Son of God might be glorified thereby," (John 11:4). Lazarus' sisters believed that Jesus could have healed their brother had He arrived in time. But Jesus waited until after Lazarus died before He stepped into the situation. Jesus told his disciples "…I am glad for your sakes that I was not there, to the intent ye may believe…" (John 11:15).

God is still a miracle-worker. He is still performing miracles. Just as Shadrach, Meshach, and Abednego trusted in the power of God, we must depend on the miracle-working power of God in times of distress. God reserves the right to come into our human affairs at any given time and do what is thought to be impossible. The crises, storms and trials of life can come in many forms, but it's good to know that our God operates in the realm of the supernatural. He is not constrained by time or space. He's sovereign. He can do whatever He wants to do whenever He wants to do it and for whomever He chooses. Children of God cannot allow the circumstances of life to change their faith in the power of God. The Lord will always have the last word. If you are presently in the midst of a serious crisis, it could be that the stage is being set for a miracle.

CAN GOD BE TRUSTED?

"Then the king commanded, and they brought Daniel, and cast him into the den of lions. Now the king spake and said unto Daniel, Thy God whom thou servest continually, he will deliver thee."

Daniel 6:16

Daniel was a man who had been diligent, faithful and fully committed to Jehovah God. He was faithful to God even in the midst of a strange land, while surrounded by strange people who embraced strange customs. He was noted as a man of great faith and one who prayed three times every day. In fact, he was so faithful to God that he would not eat anything that he thought was displeasing to God (Daniel 1:8). Daniel consecrated himself to the Lord and refused to become woven into the pagan culture of Babylon. Yet, in spite of his devotion to God, Daniel found himself in the throes of serious trouble. He was cast into a den of lions.

I found it strange and I must admit that, even as a young boy, I pondered in my own heart about this biblical episode. When one of my boyhood Sunday school teachers, the late Sister Leona Aikens, told us about Daniel's predicament, I raised the question, "If Daniel was so close to God, why would God allow something like that to happen to him? What kind of God would allow His faithful dedicated and committed servant to experience such misfortune?" This is a serious concern and I know that I'm not the only one who has wrestled with it. Maybe you have pondered this question in the secret chambers of your own mind. Maybe you never voiced it openly, but maybe you've hosted the thought in your mind. If God would allow terrible things to happen to His faithful servant, one can justifiably ask the question, "Can God be trusted?"

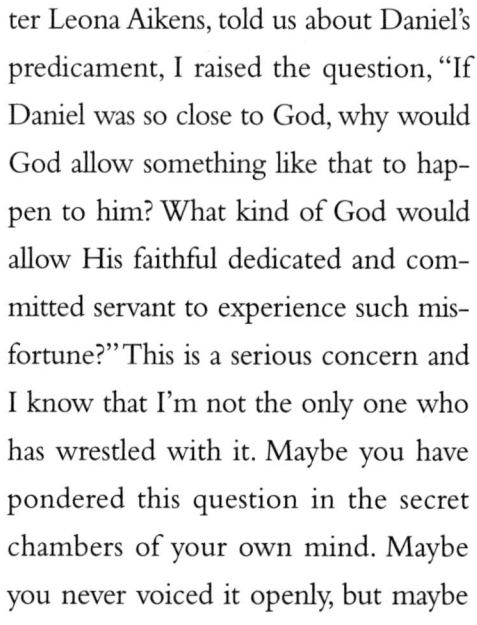

> **What kind of God would allow His faithful dedicated and committed servant to experience such misfortune?**

Say whatever you will or may, but trust is an important thing. Many relationships have failed due to the loss of trust. Love bonds spouses together. Love is to a marriage what mortar is to the bricks in a wall. But, in a marital relationship, love alone is not enough. In addition to love there must be trust. If the truth were told, many individuals who are in divorce courts across this land right now would admit that they are not there because they stopped loving each other. They are there because irreparable damage was done to the trust in the relationship.

Trust is difficult to earn and even more difficult to rebuild. In my personal dealings with people, I have reached the conclusion that no matter how much I love you, if I can't trust you, I'll always be suspicious of you. As a preacher, I've noticed that a lot of people look at me funny and seem to say, "I've heard you sing. I've heard you preach, and all of that was good but the bottom line is, can I trust you?" I understand their skepticism because a lot of people sing well and many preach well. There are many who can pray fervent prayers who are not trustworthy. Trust is important in every aspect of our lives. Even our relationship with God is contingent upon trust.

> **Trust is difficult to earn and even more difficult to rebuild.**

The text revolves around a popular biblical character. Daniel was one brought as a slave from Judah into Babylon along with a great host of others. God did great things for His faithful servant, Daniel. Daniel ascended to heights of great prestige and prominence. The record tells us that he who had once been a slave had risen to a level in the Babylonian government that was second only to King Darius. He started out a slave, but eventually ranked higher than those who had been over him. If you stay with God, He's able to take the tail and make it the head. If you stay with God, He's able to take you from the bottom and place you at the top. Such was the case with Daniel. Daniel had experienced tremendous success because of the goodness of God. God was with Daniel and there is no doubt about God being with us. The question is, are **we** with God?

I'm happy to report that not only was God with Daniel, but Daniel remained with God. Daniel remained faithful, steadfast and committed to the almighty God. Even in that strange land, Daniel kept on praying because God is not limited to any one particular place. Jesus refers to the church as the "house of prayer" (Matthew 21:13). This is true, but the church is not the only location where prayer can take place. Children of God can pray to the Father in any place and at any time. No matter where you are when you call Him, God hears your prayer!

The record tells us that there were members of the Babylonian government who were greatly disturbed by Daniel's success. Scripture tells us that some of them conspired to bring Daniel down, but they couldn't find any legitimate wrongdoing on Daniel's part (Daniel 6:4). They knew, however, that Daniel was a man of prayer. They knew that he frequently called on Jehovah God in prayer and thus they decided to go to the king and convince the king to issue a new decree. This decree would make it unlawful for anyone to pray to any god or man other than the king for a period of thirty days. For thirty whole days, no one would be able to raise a petition to any person or any god except the king. If anyone were caught praying during this period of time, they would be cast into a den of ferocious lions.

Daniel had a problem with the new edict. I can imagine that Daniel thought to himself, "Thirty days without prayer. I have to pray! Prayer places me in touch with the source of my strength. Prayer puts me in immediate contact with the One who made me. My joy comes from the Lord and, if I don't check in, I won't be able to make it." Daniel had become a prayer addict! We've all heard of crack addicts and cocaine addicts, but Daniel was addicted to prayer. Once Daniel learned that the law had taken effect, he decided that it was better to please God than to please man. Daniel went into his chambers to pray.

Daniel's enemies had him under their wicked surveillance. They knew that he prayed often and they wanted to catch him in the act of prayer. Scripture tells us that Daniel didn't change his regular routine. He went into his chamber with his window open towards Jerusalem. He prayed and gave thanks to God as he had always done (Daniel 6:10).

Daniel's private prayer meeting no doubt started with his being somewhat distracted. Would he be caught and, if so, would he meet the terrible fate dictated by the new decree? Maybe he should attempt to conceal his prayer time in some way so that others would not notice. I am sure that these distracting thoughts were short-lived as the simple act of prayer ushers us into the presence of God. In the sixteenth division of Psalms, David wrote, "In [the Lord's] presence is the fullness of joy," (Psalm 16:11). I'm certain that, once Daniel entered into the presence of God, the joy of the Lord entered in and his focus shifted beyond his immediate circumstances.

The record tells us that his enemies heard him and took Daniel before King Darius. I think that if we are going to be guilty of something, children of God should be guilty of prayer. The sad thing is that, if some Christians were arrested for praying and taken to court, many of them would be found **not guilty**. Too many of us call on the Lord only in the time of trouble. This is unfortunate because prayer is the primary form of communication between the believer and God. Prayer is also our access to the power of God. Through prayer, we are able to bring the power of God into our everyday circumstances. Prayer is like an invitation addressed to God to intervene in our human affairs.

> **Prayer is also our access to the power of God.**

According to Scripture, the king was very fond of Daniel and greatly distressed at the thought that he would suffer harm. He tried to find a way to exempt Daniel from the prescribed punishment, but to no avail. The king was unable to overturn the decree and he reluctantly gave the command that Daniel must be lead away to the den of lions.

This brings us back to our original question. Why would the Lord allow this to happen to one of his faithful and committed servants? God heard the plots. The Lord knew what the enemies were planning and still allowed extreme misfortune to befall his faithful servant. God could have stopped it. He could have nipped it in the bud.

Why does God allow people to lie on you when you're doing the best you can in the Lord's service? God has the power to strike a liar dead, but He sometimes allows liars and backbiters to use their words as weapons against His children. We are often hurt so badly by their words that it makes us sometimes wonder if God can be trusted. The Holy Spirit showed me that certain trials help us to mature in the things of God. Scripture tells us in James 1:2-4, "My brethren, count it all joy when ye fall into divers temptations; knowing this, that the trying of your faith worketh patience. But let patience have her perfect work, that ye may be perfect and entire, wanting nothing." God wants us to go beyond just being born again and grow into mature saints. One of the ways in which we become mature is through the development of perseverance through trials.

Daniel was cast into that den of lions. Come with me to that horrible place. You can smell it before you get there! There is a foul stench in the air coming from the lions' urine and feces about the floor. Be careful as you step inside as there are bones scattered about. Watch your step, because the bones of those who had preceded Daniel are strewn all about the den floor. You must also be careful not to make any sudden moves as this may cause these vicious lions to attack. What a gruesome and frightening situation for Daniel to be in.

So God allowed Daniel to be tried, convicted and sentenced to a painful death. What Daniel's enemies did not know was that God would step in and rescue his servant in a miraculous way. God dispatched an angel from Heaven. The angel's job was not to roll the stone away from the opening to the den so that Daniel might escape. The angel's assignment was not to transform the lions into harmless kittens. The angel's job was to shut the lions' jaws so that they could do Daniel no harm.

Early the next morning, the king rejoiced to discover that Daniel was still alive. When Daniel was raised up out of the den, Scripture says, "…no manner of hurt was found upon him, because he believed in his God," (Daniel 6:23). The king then commanded that Daniel's enemies be cast into the same pit from which he had emerged. Daniel's enemies were immediately destroyed.

The life of Daniel and his experience in the lions' den provide shining examples of the importance of faith. Daniel's commitment to God granted him access to God's **provision** by allowing Daniel to prosper in a strange land surrounded by his enemies. Daniel's lions' den experience also revealed two additional by-products of faith—God's **peace** and God's **protection.**

So the question on the floor is, "Can God be trusted?" The answer to this question is a resounding **Yes!** King Darius provided tremendous justification of our trust in God when he said, "…for he is the living God, and stedfast for ever, and his kingdom that which shall not be destroyed, and his dominion shall be even unto the end. He delivereth and rescueth, and he worketh signs and wonders in heaven and in earth…" (Daniel 6:26-27). Yes, our God can be trusted.

CRUCIAL FAITH FOR CRITICAL TIMES

"Then Jesus went thence, and departed into the coasts of Tyre and Sidon. And, behold, a woman of Canaan came out of the same coasts, and cried unto him, saying, Have mercy on me, O Lord, thou son of David; my daughter is grievously vexed with a devil. But he answered her not a word. And his disciples came and besought him, saying, Send her away; for she crieth after us. But he answered and said, I am not sent but unto the lost sheep of the house of Israel. Then came she and worshipped him, saying, Lord, help me. But he answered and said, It is not meet to take the children's bread, and to cast it to dogs. And she said, Truth, Lord: yet the dogs eat of the crumbs which fall from their masters' table. Then Jesus answered and said unto her, O woman, great is thy faith: be it unto thee even as thou wilt. And her daughter was made whole from that very hour."

Matthew 15:21-28

I cannot overstate the importance of faith; its worth is invaluable. I cannot quantify the significance of faith; its weight is immeasurable. Faith is crucial in the life of the believer. In critical or troubled times, faith causes us to look to the hills from whence comes our help (Psalm 121:1-2). Faith is too crucial for us to try to make it through this life without it. If we hope to gain victory over life's perils, we must have faith in our God.

The text informs us of a nameless woman who distinguished herself as a person of extraordinary faith. In fact, Jesus himself commended her for her great faith. He didn't give such praise often because He didn't often run into people with that level of faith. Her encounter with Jesus became one of three instances recorded in Scripture when the Savior commended individuals for their faith.

On one such occasion, Jesus commended the faith of a centurion who was seeking help for his young servant. To paraphrase their conversation the centurion said to Jesus: "I'm not worthy for you to come under my roof, but I believe that you can speak a word right where you are and the situation at my house will change. You've got so much power that you don't even have to be on the premises in order to make a difference in my situation." Jesus granted his request and commended him saying: "I have not found so great faith, no, not in Israel" (Matthew 8:5-10).

Another occasion when the Master commended a person of great faith was when a woman sought healing for "an issue of blood" that she had suffered with for twelve years. When she heard that Jesus was in town, she was determined to receive her miracle. She concluded in her own heart, "If I may touch but his clothes, I shall be whole," (Mark 5:28). When she made contact with the hem of His garment, scripture says Jesus stopped for a moment and asked, "Who touched my clothes?" (Mark 5:30). After the woman identified herself as the one who touched Him, Jesus said, "Daughter, thy faith hath made thee whole…" (Mark 5:34). Jesus credited her faith as being the catalyst for her miraculous recovery.

Prior to the time of our text, Jesus arrived at the coasts of Tyre and Sidon (Matthew 15:21). It is reported in the gospel of Mark, that the Master tried to conceal the fact that He was coming (Mark 7:24). He arrived unannounced, but Jesus' presence is like the fragrance of sweet perfume. When a sweet fragrance is in the air, it won't take long before everyone knows it. The word got out that Jesus was in the area. Scripture noted that among those who learned of His presence was a mother who was in a critical time in her life. I have no problem relating to her for I have lived long enough to know something about critical times. Critical times can be overwhelming. If there is ever a time when faith is important, it is in the midst of critical times. We should never enter a critical time faithless for, if we do, we might end up making unwise decisions. In the midst of critical times, those with

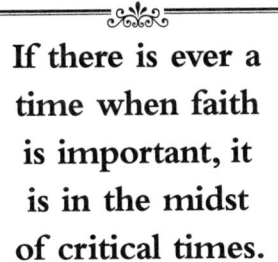

> **If there is ever a time when faith is important, it is in the midst of critical times.**

little or no faith might entertain the idea of giving up. They may even entertain thoughts of taking their own lives simply because the times are critical and they are without faith.

The woman in our text was in the midst of a critical period or time. When she learned about Jesus, she considered herself fortunate. She probably thought, "Oh, how blessed I am. I couldn't get to Him, but He's now come to me. He's in my neck of the woods." Jesus has a way of drawing close to those who are in the midst of critical times. She did not send for Him. He just showed up. He knows what we need even before we ask Him (Matthew 6:8).

Scripture tells us that the woman made her way to Jesus. She had not gotten on His itinerary; she just came to where He was. Following behind Him and His disciples, she raised her voice to the point that everyone could hear her. As she followed Him, she cried out saying, "Have mercy on me, O Lord, thou son of David; my daughter is grievously vexed with a devil." She prayed with sincerity. She prayed fervently from the depths of her heart. I've come to discover that our prayers don't have to be long to be effective. A prayer does not have to be lengthy to beget powerful results. The woman called out to Jesus and He heard her but He did not immediately respond.

Though He kept walking seemingly ignoring her call, the woman decided to keep following Him. Here is a test for us. How many times have we called Him and seemingly received no response? We must not give up on the Lord because He does not answer right away. We must not be too hasty and give up on the Master and on His deliverance because He has not yet responded to our prayer. You may have been praying and talking to the Lord, and it seems that no response has come. However, there is good news. He heard the call, and He will respond! God's delay must not be mistaken for a denial. He doesn't operate on our time. The challenge for us is to hold firmly to our faith when we go through a period when it seems that the answers to our prayers are not coming right away. Many of us miss out on blessings, not because we did not pray, but because we gave up too quickly! If we call Him once and He does not seem respond, we must continue to follow Him and call Him again. If this ancient report teaches anything, it is that persistence begets blessings.

Jesus' disciples became impatient with the woman. I don't know why they had a problem with her. She wasn't calling them! I don't know why they got upset. She wasn't asking them to help her. She was asking Jesus to help her! Seeing someone else call on the Lord often aggravates some people. If someone wants to call on the Lord, all others should do their best to not interfere. Onlookers should make every attempt to not be a hindrance when another is attempting to communicate with the Giver of every good and perfect gift (James 1:17). This was not the case with the disciples. They complained to Jesus about the woman and asked Him to send her away.

This mother had a child that was vexed with a demon. Scripture doesn't go into detail as to how badly the child was afflicted. Obviously the child was greatly tormented, so much so that it troubled the heart of the mother. Then, interestingly enough, Jesus stopped and said, "It is not meet (or appropriate) to take the children's bread and cast it to dogs." One might wonder why the Lord spoke to the woman so harshly. Knowledge of the culture in that part of the world, during that period in history, leads to understanding. Jews considered Gentiles, who were also referred to as non-Jews, as no better than dogs. Similarly, many Gentiles despised Jews. Jesus used language that was expected between Jews and Gentiles during those days; thereby He created the woman's greatest test of faith. The quality of one's faith cannot be determined until it is tested. Many of us are walking around thinking we have faith, but only when it is tested by critical times, do we discover our true level of faith.

Jesus spoke bluntly to the woman, but she did not let pride deter her. She did not become distracted with feelings of insult. She remained steadfast in her resolve and firm in her faith. She addressed the dog issue directly by saying, in essence, "Alright, Master, you spoke about dogs and it not being appropriate to give the children's bread to dogs. Let me say something about dogs. Good masters always have some scraps for the dogs. I don't argue or debate my being a dog, but since you are The Good Master, I'm just asking for a few scraps!" Jesus turned and spoke to her, "Woman, great is thy faith." He assured her that everything that she had asked for would be given her all because of her faith. She had crucial faith for a critical time.

Faith is necessary so that if the times in our lives should suddenly become critical, our faith will sustain us. What I love about faith during difficult situations is that faith becomes verbal. Our faith can carry on a conversation with us in the midst of critical times. During the most difficult circumstances, our faith will tell us, "I know it's dark. It doesn't take a rocket scientist to figure out that you're in serious trouble, but don't throw in the towel! Don't give up! Don't throw up your hands! Just hold on a little while longer!" Faith reminds us that sorrow is going to turn into joy, weakness into strength, and midnight into high noon.

> **Our faith can carry on a conversation with us in the midst of critical times.**

When the woman got home, she found that what Jesus had promised had indeed been done. Before she got there, the blessing had already arrived. In other words, the breakthrough beat the woman home. I do not know whether she walked, jogged or ran but I do know, according to scripture, when she got home the blessing was already there. When the woman got home, her daughter had been made well. She already had been made whole. She was lying on top of the bed, and was no longer vexed. The devil had fled.

I thank God that, when He moves, things change. When God moves, things are no longer the same. Children of God must have faith and know that, though the situation is critical, nothing is too hard for God. If we have crucial faith during our critical times, our faith will sustain us and eventually bring about our deliverance.

A FAITH THAT WILL NOT QUIT

"And again he entered into Capernaum after some days; and it was noised that he was in the house. And straightway many were gathered together, insomuch that there was no room to receive them, no, not so much as about the door: and he preached the word unto them. And they come unto him, bringing one sick of the palsy, which was borne of four. And when they could not come nigh unto him for the press, they uncovered the roof where he was: and when they had broken it up, they let down the bed wherein the sick of the palsy lay. When Jesus saw their faith, he said unto the sick of the palsy, Son, thy sins be forgiven thee."

Mark 2: 1-5

The text opens with Jesus once again coming to the city of Capernaum. Jesus had had some unpleasant experiences in His hometown, Nazareth. He experienced tremendous hostility in His own hometown and was the victim of scorn and ridicule at the hands of His own countrymen. Consequently, Jesus moved

His base of operation from Nazareth to Capernaum. From this ancient account, we learn that, when faced with rejection, children of God should not be deterred. We must keep traveling the path prescribed by His will and live for Him in order to fulfill God's purpose for our lives.

Nazareth's loss became Capernaum's gain. Jesus received a warm reception in Capernaum. The citizens of Capernaum had grown accustomed to walking and talking with Jesus. They had grown accustomed to sitting in His presence and enjoying His fellowship. They had received many blessings while in His presence; so they were glad that Jesus was back in town.

Permit me to say that there was no televised announcement of His return. There were no radios on which to broadcast the fact that He was back. There was no daily newspaper to publish the fact that He had returned. The good news of the Master's return spread by word of mouth. Men and women came from all around to the small house where Jesus was. The crowd completely filled the house where our Savior was, and those who could not get in jammed the doorway. The text explained that there was no room left for anyone else to access the house by way of the door.

The record further tells of a very sad case. We are told of a man who was not identified by name but rather by condition. He was a sick man ailing with the palsy. His condition had grown so severe that he had been rendered unable to walk. Because he could not do for himself, he was dependent upon others to do for him.

This man didn't have many things, but he did have friends. We should carry ourselves in such a way that we can at least have a few friends. Scripture tells us, "If you desire friends you ought show yourself friendly," (Proverbs 18:24). I have traveled all over this nation, and I have met so many unfriendly people. I have met so many bitter people. It is a sad testimony to a good God. If we serve a God that is as good as we say He is, we ought to be able to smile sometimes.

The feeble man in our text had friends. We know they were real friends by virtue of what they did for the ailing man. According to Scripture, four men were seriously concerned about their friend and were intent on getting him to Jesus. I can imagine that, in their dialogue with one another, they shared these thoughts: "The Wonder-Worker is back! This would be a prime opportunity for us to get our sick brother to Jesus. We don't have the remedy for his condition, but we know who does. Let's get our friend to Jesus."

We find out who our real friends are in our time of need.

We find out who our real friends are in our time of need. Frequent visits are not a gauge for true friendship. The person who visits you most can prove to be your worst enemy. Frequent phone calls also are not a good measure of true friendship because the person who engages us in conversation most frequently could be gathering information to use against us one day. The four men in our text were true friends of the ailing man, because they put their agendas on hold for him. They were moved by such compassion for the man that they stopped what they were doing to help him.

I submit to you that the faith of these men was such that they knew that their journey was going to be a one-way trip of sorts. They knew that they would have to carry their friend to Jesus, but, after receiving a deliverance from Jesus, their friend could carry himself home. They picked him up—bed and all—and started carrying him to Jesus.

It's good that the ailing man had four friends, because the bed had four corners. There was a friend for every corner. There was help for every need. Every corner was covered. This story parallels the roles of each member of the Body of Christ. In the Body of Christ, there are many corners that need to be carried. If any member is not carrying a corner, then some aspect of the work of the church is sorely lacking or left undone. One's corner may be on the Usher Board. Another's corner may be in the choir. Still another's corner may be the Sunday School Department or Youth Department. But whatever our ministry or calling may be, each of us must identify and work in our specific area of service. The burden is not as heavy when each of us carries our own corner. One of the things that hinders church work is that there are so few who actually carry a corner. In this passage, however, each friend carried a corner.

The journey continued until they arrived at the house where Jesus was. When they got there, however, they were met with an unexpected setback. They could not get in. The entrance was blocked and no one was willing to move aside and allow them room to get their sick friend through. At this point, they could have thrown up their hands, turned to their sick buddy and said: "Oh well, we tried. We gave it our best shot, but we can't get you in. Maybe on some future occasion we'll have opportunity to get you to Jesus." Such was not the case with these four men. They possessed a faith that would not quit. Their engines were fueled by a faith that told them, "Where there is a will; there is a way." Their faith would not allow them to give up. According to Scripture, they climbed onto the rooftop. The record is that when they got up there they began to tear a hole in the roof. They had the audacity to tear a hole in somebody else's roof! They tore a hole in the roof large enough for their sick friend's body to pass through. They were determined to get their sick friend in to see Jesus. They lowered him down through that hole in the roof.

Their chief desire was to see their friend raised up, but before he could be raised up, he first had to be lowered down. A great many people in the church have trouble being raised up because they are not humble enough to lower themselves down. They lowered him down, and the people in the house saw him coming through the rooftop. Everybody's eyes gazed up at the man coming through the roof. However, Scripture tells us that, despite the extraordinary, even astonishing actions of these men, Jesus recognized more about

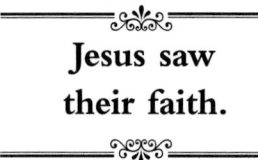

Jesus saw their faith.

them. Jesus saw their faith. They had climbed on top of another man's house, tore a hole in the roof so large that a man could fit through it and lowered their friend down into a crowded room. Nevertheless, what Jesus saw was their **faith**.

Jesus saw their faith and said to the invalid, "Son, thy sins be forgiven." He went on to say, "Arise, and take up thy bed, and go thy way into thine house," (Mark 2:11). The man rose immediately, took up his bed and walked out of the house to the amazement of all that were gathered there. After witnessing this miracle, the crowd glorified God.

The faith of the four men was such that it motivated the Master to work a wonder in the life of a man who was in a tragic condition. Jesus was motivated to do for a man what He very possibly would not have done were it not for his friends' display of faith. Their faith endured setbacks. Their faith endured hardships, barriers, and obstacles. Their faith in the power of God was so great that they would stop at nothing to get to Jesus. Truly, their faith was a faith that would not quit.

> **Faith makes the difference between success and failure in the life of the believer.**

As children of God, we should all endeavor to have this kind of faith. Faith makes the difference between success and failure in the life of the believer. Faith makes the difference between victory and defeat. We will suffer many challenges to our faith in the form of setbacks, disappointments and outright failure, but we must persevere in spite of these obstacles in order to live victoriously. If we are to live victoriously, we must have a faith that will not quit.

THE AWESOME POWER OF PRAYER

"Turn again, and tell Hezekiah the captain of my people, Thus saith the LORD, the God of David thy father, I have heard thy prayer, I have seen thy tears: behold, I will heal thee: on the third day thou shalt go up unto the house of the LORD. And I will add unto thy days fifteen years; and I will deliver thee and this city out of the hand of the king of Assyria; and I will defend this city for mine own sake, and for my servant David's sake."

II Kings 20:5-6

The message in this text is the second one that God sent to King Hezekiah by way of the prophet Isaiah, and the second message is far different from the first. In the first message, God instructs Isaiah to tell Hezekiah to set his house in order because he is going to die and not live, but very shortly thereafter God speaks to the prophet and, in essence, tells him, "Turn, go back and tell Hezekiah that I'm going to grant him fifteen more years."

The questions to consider are: "What accounts for the sudden shift? What caused God to change his mind?" The answers are quite simple. Between the first message and the second message, **Hezekiah prayed!** Between message number one and message number two, Hezekiah turned his face to the wall, and cried out to God in prayer. Prayer can make the difference when nothing else can.

> **Prayer can make the difference when nothing else can.**

This ancient report is just one of many examples in Scripture of the awesome power of prayer. The tremendous agony and trials of Job were changed for the better after Job prayed (Job 42:10). The rebellious prophet Jonah was delivered from the belly of the great fish after he prayed (Jonah 2). God rained down a consuming fire, on the top of Mount Carmel after the prophet Elijah prayed (I Kings 18:36-38). Because of the prayers of the saints, Peter was delivered from prison by an angel of the Lord (Acts 12:5-11). Deliverance came to Paul and Silas when they were unjustly imprisoned in a Philippian jail. At midnight, they had a two-man prayer session during which they prayed and sang praises to God. God sent a great earthquake that shook the foundation of the prison. The doors of the prison were opened, they were loosed from their shackles and they were delivered (Acts 16:22-36). Prayer is a powerful thing.

I cannot overemphasize the important role of prayer in the lives of believers. Prayer is our means of communicating with

God. Through effective prayer, we acquire the spiritual strength needed to be effective in every area of life.

Scripture stresses the importance of prayer. Prayer plays such a vital role in sustaining the believer that Jesus, through the use of a parable, encouraged His disciples to always pray and not faint (Luke 18:1-8). In this passage of Scripture, Jesus teaches His disciples that God will avenge those who cry unto Him day and night. We are also told in Scripture, "…The effectual fervent prayer of a righteous man availeth much," (James 5:16). Effectual prayer is based on one's faith in the power of God.

> **Through effective prayer, we acquire the spiritual strength needed to be effective in every area of life.**

God acts on our behalf every time we pray even when it seems that our prayer is ineffective in achieving the desired result. An immediate change may not take place in our situation, but God is at work. So often, we grow weary while waiting for God to move in a given situation but God sustains us during times of waiting. He keeps us from being overtaken by adversity and, if we keep our minds on Him, He has promised us perfect peace (Isaiah 26:3). Think about the many times that you would have been swept away in the midst of a difficult time had it not been for God's sustaining power. This power comes about when we pray. Prayer is never a wasted effort. Sincere prayer is never a useless exercise.

One of the beautiful things about prayer is that no special occasion or situation is necessary for prayer to take place. Prayer can go forth without anything being wrong. While there are prayers of urgency when we need God's help in a hurry, there are prayers of thanksgiving and prayers of communion during which times we are blessed to engage in dialogue with the Almighty.

There have been times when I have tried to reach others and found reaching them to be difficult and sometimes impossible. Sometimes, in the times of hardship and difficulty when we really need someone to talk to, we may find it difficult to reach anyone. Thus, conversation at a needed time could not take place. Our God, however, is accessible, available, and reachable. Calling Him through prayer never bothers Him. Whenever we call God, He is always glad to hear from us. God delights in hearing from His children.

What a marvelous thing it is that we have the ability to reach heavenly headquarters at times when we cannot reach others. How wonderful it is to know that when we call God, we won't get an answering service. We get Him! Every time we pray, we can reach heaven and communicate with God, which is no small privilege. How important would we consider it if we could reach the President of the United States when we called him? How valuable would we rate the privilege of being able to communicate with other high-ranking government officials? How much more privileged are we that we can reach God?

Unfortunately, in many Christian circles, prayer has become

minimized—almost trivialized. Some of us think that prayer is some little thing that we do in times of distress, but prayer must be viewed as an awesome act, as a thing that moves God. When we encounter a friend or loved one who is going through a tough time we often say, "I'll pray for you" because we think it is the appropriate thing to say. However, we must remain mindful of the fact that when we pray we make contact with the most powerful force in the Universe, and prayer can make all the difference.

I thank God for the awesome power and privilege of prayer. I've discovered that prayer accomplishes at least two things. Prayer *repairs* and prayer *prepares*. When we pray, wounded spirits are repaired and broken hearts are restored. God's healing power is released when we pray. Prayer also prepares us for challenges and opportunities that lie ahead. When we are in constant communication with the Father, we receive guidance through His Holy Spirit that allows us to avoid pitfalls and take advantage of God-given opportunities. When we are faced with challenges and decisions in life, we must pray so that God will strengthen and guide us along the way.

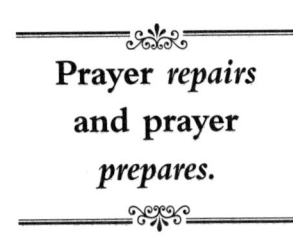

> **Prayer *repairs* and prayer *prepares*.**

The man of our text, King Hezekiah, was a man who could speak from personal experience about the awesome power of prayer. At the time of our text, the nation of Israel had been divided into two kingdoms: the northern kingdom and the southern kingdom. The northern kingdom retained the name Israel, and the southern kingdom was named Judah. Hezekiah was the King of Judah. Unlike many of his predecessors, King Hezekiah was a good king. King Hezekiah tore down the statues of idol gods and led the people to worship the true and living God. But God has now sent him word, "…thou shalt die, and not live," (II Kings 20:1).

Permit me to say that Hezekiah was a good man, but good people are not exempt from trouble. Trouble has come directly to the good king's palace. King Hezekiah was a wealthy and powerful man, but trouble does not discriminate. Trouble comes to the rich as well as the poor. Trouble comes to those of great influence as well as those with little clout. Trouble comes to people of all races and nationalities. If we live long enough in this world, trouble will come to us.

The king himself is now on his bed of affliction. The king himself is now a victim of serious illness. According to the record, he is sick, and his sickness has taken such a toll upon him physically until he is no longer able to sit on the royal throne. He is now confined to his bed. Scripture informs us that a strange boil appeared on the body of King Hezekiah. He sent for the best medical experts of his day. Hezekiah had the money to pay them for the medical treatment he needed, but none of their ointments or salves proved to be effective. Charles Spurgeon, the great British theologian, suggests that every day the boil increased in size and increased in depth. It became

The Awesome Power of Prayer

so painful to Hezekiah until his movement had now become restricted. Whenever he moved, he felt great pain coming from that hideous boil. Some say that the boil had grown passed the size of a large plate. His condition was extremely serious. We never know what condition we will end up in before we leave this world. Hezekiah was at the point of death.

Now, as Hezekiah's struggle continued, God talks to the prophet, Isaiah, and tells him to go to King Hezekiah with news that will be even the more disturbing. He tells Isaiah to tell the king, "Thus saith the LORD, Set thine house in order; for thou shalt die, and not live," (II Kings 20:1). In other words, the prophet is to warn the king to get his affairs in order because he is going to die. God is gracious enough to give Hezekiah advanced warning.

King Hezekiah and the prophet Isaiah were good friends. It's a wonderful thing when government and religious figures can enjoy friendship. It is wonderful when politics and righteousness can enjoy camaraderie and harmony. Hezekiah was Isaiah's friend, and Isaiah hated to trouble his friend at a time when he was already down.

Deitrich Bonhoeffer, the German theologian, suggests that, when Hezekiah learned that the prophet Isaiah had arrived at the palace, Hezekiah was happy and optimistic about what the Lord might say about his condition. I can imagine him saying to himself, "Maybe this is going to be the news that I have been waiting on. Maybe my friend the prophet is coming to bring exciting news of what God is going to do and how He is going to deliver me from this crisis." No doubt Hezekiah was devastated to hear the heartbreaking news. The news caused even more hurt and even more pain to a man who was already down. Isaiah did not stay after he delivered the message. He left the room and started making his way out of the palace.

Hezekiah made a powerful conscious decision. He decided to have prayer. Scripture says that he turned his face to the wall and talked to God in prayer. The scholars suggest that he turned to the wall because King Hezekiah's royal attendants were in the room, but there was nobody between Hezekiah and the wall.

I thank God for the people in my life who pray for me. I sincerely believe that I have experienced tremendous breakthroughs and been delivered from countless trials because of the fervent prayers of believers, but it is crucial that children of God learn to pray for themselves. It is a wonderful thing to know for yourself that God hears and answers prayer.

When we truly want to reach God in prayer, sometimes we have to turn away from others and focus on God. Hezekiah turned. God became the center of his focus. Nobody else was on his mind but God. If we want to pray effectively, we must put all other things aside and focus on God alone. Our focus must be on the Almighty!

Hezekiah had a one-man prayer meeting. It doesn't take a large number of people to have effective prayer. I love to pray with other believers, but some of my most effective times in prayer have been when I have been all by myself. When I am by myself, I can talk to Him about private, personal matters that I dare not address in the presence of others! Some things are too sensitive. Some things are too delicate. Some things are too intimate and too personal to talk about in front of anyone else!

Hezekiah talked to God. Permit me to paraphrase this powerful prayer. King Hezekiah said, "Lord, don't you remember how I walked with you? Don't you remember how I talked with you? Don't you remember how I lived for you and how I've encouraged others to walk with you?" Hezekiah kept on "Lord, I know the message you sent, but, Lord, I have one request to make. Lord, give me just a little more time." King Hezekiah prayed so fervently that tears ran from his eyes

God heard Hezekiah's prayer. The record tells us that before the prophet Isaiah had even gotten out of the palace, God spoke to him and said, "Turn again, and tell Hezekiah the, captain of my people, Thus saith the LORD, the God of David thy father, I have heard thy prayer, I have seen thy tears: behold, I will heal thee: on the third day thou shalt go up unto the house of the LORD. And I will add unto thy days fifteen years; and I will deliver thee and this city out of the hand of the king of Assyria; and I will defend this city for mine own sake, and for my servant David's sake," (II Kings 20:5-6). When Isaiah delivered the news, it was a time of rejoicing and celebration. The record tells us that three days later Hezekiah made his way up to the house of the Lord and worshipped Him.

This episode of Hezekiah's life truly demonstrates the awesome power of prayer. Hezekiah's prayer moved the heart of God and not only did God heal Hezekiah's condition and extend his life, but this powerful prayer also moved God to defend Hezekiah's kingdom from her enemies. God showed Himself strong on Hezekiah's behalf because he prayed. King Hezekiah, in turn, went to the temple to offer praises to God.

As children of God, prayer should always be our first response to adversity. As demonstrated by this and other biblical accounts, effective prayers move not only the heart of God but also the hand of God. Sometimes, however, God doesn't move as we might anticipate. It is, therefore, incumbent upon the believer to have faith not only in the power of God to bring about a change but also the wisdom of God to know how best to orchestrate the situations of our lives to our benefit. We gain access to this through our faith and the awesome power of prayer.

Part Three:

The *Must* of Victorious Living

Introduction

Receiving salvation through the Lord Jesus Christ re-establishes the broken relationship between God and man. We have been brought out of darkness into the marvelous light of the Gospel of Jesus Christ. Our spirits have been made alive in Christ. Nevertheless, a separation of sorts still exists because our old mindsets and ways of doing things aren't compatible with our new lives in Christ. But our God is a loving God. The Word of God as revealed to us by the Holy Spirit shows us the areas in our lives that are not pleasing to God and gently guides us to repentance. As we bring our faults before the Lord and mature in the things of God, our conversations, relationships, lifestyles, behavior and decisions conform more and more to the will of God.

The will of God has not changed since creation. When God created man, He created him in His own image (Genesis 1:27). After sin entered in, Jesus came to restore mankind back to the Father. This restoration consists not only of salvation, but a complete spiritual transformation into the image of Christ. The apostle Paul wrote, "For whom he did foreknow, he also did predestinate to be conformed to the image of his Son, that he might be the firstborn among many brethren" (Romans 8:29). The process of becoming Christ-like occurs gradually as we move from one level of spiritual growth to the next.

How are we being transformed into Christ's image? It all starts in the mind. We are transformed into the image of Christ as our minds are renewed through the Word of God. Ephesians 4:22-24 instructs us to put off the old man and put on the new man by being "...renewed in the spirit of your mind." Romans 12:2 issues a warning not to conform our lives to worldly standards, but to be "...transformed by the renewing of your mind." This verse goes on to say that by renewing our minds we are then able to prove the perfect will of God for our lives. In doing so, we bring honor and glory to God.

THE IMPORTANCE OF RIGHT CHOICES

"Behold, I set before you this day a blessing and a curse; A blessing, if ye obey the commandments of the Lord your God, which I command you this day. And a curse, if ye will not obey the commandments of the Lord your God, but turn aside out of the way which I command you this day, to go after other gods, which ye have not known."

Deuteronomy 11:26-28

We are introduced to the matter of choice early in life. At an early age we receive praise when we make a good behavior choice. On the other hand, many times we received punishment when we made the wrong choice. I was raised by both my mother and grandmother. Even in my early boyhood, they refused to remove the decorative pieces, or "what-nots" as my grandmother called them, from the tables. They chose to leave the various statuettes where they were and told me not to touch them. Needless to say, I learned early on that to bother certain things would constitute a bad choice. In this and many other circumstances, I learned that to defy instructions would result in terrible and even painful consequences. My mother and grandmother had not read any of Dr. Spock's books on proper child rearing, but they knew what worked!

We are faced with choices every day of our lives. What should I wear? What should I eat? We're faced with choices on every hand. Some choices are more crucial than others because some of our choices will have a great impact on our future. Choices that we make at critical junctures in our lives must not be taken lightly for these choices can affect us tomorrow, next year and even forever.

So many people are agonizing today over circumstances resulting from the bad choices that they made in the past. A bad choice can do so much damage and prove to be so destructive. So powerful is this simple thing called choice.

So many negative life experiences can be avoided by making right choices. Many times our own personal beds are made hard to sleep in because we made the wrong choice. The wrong choice caused the first man and woman to be expelled from that garden paradise called Eden (Genesis 3). It was a wrong choice that caused Samson to be blinded by his enemies (Judges 16). It was the wrong choice that caused David to sin greatly before Jehovah (II Samuel 11). Wrong choices often carry heavy penalties. Even after receiving God's forgiveness, many times the consequences of a bad choice remain.

God has made us creatures of choice. As it relates to our personal lives, He has given us the ability and the privilege to make choices. Even when it comes to God Himself, He does not force Himself upon us but grants each one of us the privilege to choose.

> **Even after receiving God's forgiveness, many times the consequences of a bad choice remain.**

Early in my Christian walk, I questioned why the Lord would leave important life decisions in the hands of fallible men. Why did He grant us so much leverage? Since He's omniscient, He knew what man would do from the very beginning. He knew the mistakes that we would make before the doctor spanked our bottoms and we cried our first cry in this realm of humanity. He knew the wrong turns we would take. Why would He grant man all of this freedom knowing that, on many occasions, man would be guilty of making the wrong choices? The Holy Spirit helped me out greatly and gave me the following response: God made man a creature of choice because God wants man to serve Him not by force, but by choice.

God could have programmed us like man programs computers or robots. However, God gets no glory from anything that is forced. God wants us to come to Him by choice. When we come to Him by choice, the songs that we sing bring glory to Him. The sermons we preach and the service we render bring glory to God because, despite the divine call on our lives, we are doing all of these things by choice. Our service to God should not be drudgery. Our service to God should be done with a grateful heart in a spirit of excellence because we serve an excellent God.

Our text provides a vivid demonstration of the importance of making the right choice. Permit me to paraphrase our text. Moses told the children of Israel, "What I set before you this day are actually the commandments, the laws, and the statues of God." He further suggests, "Now it will be a blessing for those who obey the laws and statues of God, but it will be a curse for those who choose to disobey." So, our choices determine whether or not the truth of God proves to be a blessing or a curse, and since we have been given this privilege of choice, we must choose wisely.

> **God wants us to come to Him by choice.**

Even today we have a choice. We can choose to live according to our own ways or live in accordance with the will of God. If we hear God's voice and choose our own way, we are on a path that leads to our own destruction. If we choose to receive and apply God's principles to our lives, we become recipients of great benefits and blessings.

So many Christians have been operating under a false assumption concerning the promises of God. Many well-meaning Christians believe that they can be the beneficiaries of God's promises without any effort on their part. I submit to you that the promises of God are balanced. We often hear that we should "prosper and be in health," but that verse qualifies this by saying that our prosperity and health are contingent upon our souls prospering in the things of God, (III John 1:2). In the area of tithes and offerings, the book of Malachi clearly states that obedience to God's command will result in a blessing. God promises to pour out blessings that we will not have room enough to receive, (Malachi 3:10). He also promises divine protection from financial ruin, (Malachi 3:11). The ninth verse of this same chapter, however, states that those who fail to obey God in the area of tithes are "cursed with a curse." In this regard, the law of God can serve as either a blessing or a curse depending on individual choice. The same holds true as it relates to salvation through our Lord Jesus Christ. It is one Gospel, but two totally different results depending on one's choice. As children who have been exposed to the truth, we will determine whether the Gospel proves to be a blessing or a curse. Our choice will make the difference.

> **As children who have been exposed to the truth, we will determine whether the Gospel proves to be a blessing or a curse.**

When it comes to the Gospel, it is better never to hear the truth than to hear it and continue to make the wrong choices. As a preacher of the Gospel of Jesus Christ, I have become an enemy to those who walk in disobedience. Many times the messages that I preach don't sit too well with people who don't want to change. The Holy Spirit has charged me to tell others that we cannot continue to be exposed to the Word of God and continue with business as usual! The Holy Spirit is issuing a warning. You are placing your future in jeopardy if you continue to make ungodly choices. God is not pleased with Christians who continue to drink excessively, use drugs or engage in homosexuality, fornication or adultery. God is also not pleased with dishonest and immoral Christians. Dishonesty in the workplace or in business is not acceptable for a child of God. God's desire is that we exhibit godly character in all areas of our lives. Scripture informs us that "[God] hath saved us, and called us with an holy calling, not according to our works, but according to his own purpose and grace, which was given us in Christ Jesus before the world began" (II Timothy 1:9). Scripture also instructs Children of God to walk worthy of this holy calling (Ephesians 4:1).

Our Heavenly Father gives clear instructions concerning how to make the correct life choices. Jehovah has given us a list of godly principles that should govern the life of every believer. In addition, God has given us His Holy Spirit who guides us into all truth, (John 16:13). As a result, we don't have to be in a state of confusion regarding the path our lives should take. The best place for any believer to be is in the center of God's will. Proverbs 3:6 commands each of us to acknowledge God in all of our decisions and He will direct our paths.

CHECK YOUR CROWD

"Now his parents went to Jerusalem every year at the feast of the passover. And when he was twelve years old, they went up to Jerusalem after the custom of the feast. [43] And when they had fulfilled the days, as they returned, the child of Jesus tarried behind in Jerusalem; and Joseph and his mother knew not of it. [44] But they, supposing him to have been in the company, went a day's journey; and they sought him among their kinsfolk and acquaintance."

Luke 2: 41-44

Joseph and Mary have just made a troubling discovery. They have been traveling without Jesus. They've been on the road thinking that He was with them, but they have made a false assumption. They learned of this after they decided to check their crowd. I submit to you that it is imperative on the part of all believers that we first examine ourselves. Then we must take a close look at those with whom we associate. We must seriously evaluate the company we keep. We've all made mistakes. God knows I've made my share. But one of the most tragic mistakes that anyone can make is to be a part of a "Christ-less Crowd."

Mary, the mother of Jesus, and Joseph, her husband, have been to Jerusalem in observance of the feast of the Passover. The feast of the Passover was a period of seven days on the Jewish calendar when devout Jews commemorated the deliverance of Israel from bondage in Egypt.

> **We must seriously evaluate the company we keep.**

When Israel was still in bondage in Egypt, the Lord sent a series of plagues, the last of which was the death of the firstborn of every Egyptian from the firstborn of Pharaoh to the firstborn of a slave even including livestock, (Exodus 11:4-5). The Children of Israel were spared the agony of this plague because Jehovah had a plan. God's plan for the Children of Israel was for each household to kill and eat a one-year-old male lamb that was without spot or blemish. They were further instructed to sprinkle the blood of the spotless lamb on the tops and sides of the doorposts of their houses. The Lord told Moses that the blood shall be "a token," indicating that the home was to be *passed over*, (Exodus 12:13). The Lord also commanded the Children of Israel to commemorate their emancipation from Egypt throughout all generations with a seven-day feast commonly referred to as the Feast of the Passover or the Feast of Unleavened Bread, (Exodus 12:14-15). This great observance was marked by the eating of unleavened bread and special meat prepared with bitter herbs.

You and I are alive today because of some passovers. Death is all around us. Aren't you glad that when death threatened to overtake you, God's divine protection caused the Angel of Death to pass you over? We must realize that we're not here because we've been so good. We're still here because Jehovah is good. We're still alive because Jehovah has been gracious and merciful enough to cause some passovers.

> **God always has a plan. He always has a way of escape.**

God's plan was the only thing sparing the Children of Israel from this horrible plague. Jehovah had a plan. I think I ought to tell that when it comes to His beloved children, God always has a plan. He always has a way of escape. If you stay close to Him, He'll tip you off when tragedy is on the way. If you stay close to Him, He'll make you aware when crisis is about to come. As a result of God's divine direction, so many of us have avoided tragedy because we didn't make certain decisions that would have proven hazardous or even fatal. We'll never know all of the tragedies that we have avoided as a result of a Heavenly tip.

Mary and Joseph have joined in with other Jews from Nazareth forming a great multitude of travelers to Jerusalem. They enjoyed their time in Jerusalem going from one celebration to another. Now it must be mentioned that as a Jew, you could go to the Feast of the Passover, stay a few days and leave early. Mary and Joseph, however, fulfilled all seven days. In other words they put in some time that they didn't have to put in at the temple. Make up your mind that it's right to spend some time at the temple. I get so much from hanging around the temple. My bowed-down head is lifted and burdens are taken from my shoulders just as a result of being at the temple.

Now the record tells us that when their days were fulfilled, they and the multitude with them departed. Mary and Joseph are headed home. Their minds and thoughts are now on home. They had a good time at the temple. They had a good time at the feast, but it is time to go home. As they departed Jerusalem, Mary and Joseph assumed that Jesus was with them.

It never ceases to amaze me how we take so many important things for granted. I discovered early on in my Christian walk not to mistake outward religious signs as an indication of one's commitment to Christ. There's a difference between religion and relationship. The Lord is calling for relationship. He wants you to have a relationship with Him so that even when you are at home, you're throwing kisses to Him. Your relationship with God should be such that you go through each day looking for ways to honor Him. You should desire to honor Him in your conversation, conduct and service.

> **There's a difference between religion and relationship. The Lord is calling for relationship.**

We must also surround ourselves with those who have made a similar commitment to Christ. We are instructed in Scripture to "…believe not every spirit, but try the spirits whether they are of God…" (I John 4:1). Outward expressions alone are not sufficient for Jesus Himself said that a certain crowd would honor Him with their lips but their hearts would be far from Him, (Matthew 15:8).

We must show kindness to everyone but be very selective about those whom we embrace as friends. We shouldn't be selective in choosing those to whom we show kindness but we must carefully choose our close friends and companions. Scripture says, "Can two walk together, except they be agreed?" (Amos 3:3). The people that we choose as companions do one of two things: they either bring us closer to God or they cause us to drift farther away from God. In our Christian walk, we are either moving forward or going backwards. Nothing stays the same. Can Christ be found in your friends' conversations and lifestyle choices? Can Christ be found in the activities that your crowd engages in?

> **In our Christian walk, we are either moving forward or going backwards. Nothing stays the same.**

Scripture tells us that Mary and Joseph had gone a whole day's journey before they discovered that Jesus was missing. Now come a little closer. Who are these people who are unaware of the absence of Jesus? Who are these individuals who are clueless concerning the Master's absence? Who are these individuals who have just assumed that the Master was with them? Mary and Joseph.

There were also two groups mentioned with whom Mary and Joseph didn't find Jesus: kinsfolk and acquaintances. They discovered that Jesus was not in the crowd. Mary and Joseph were in a "Christ-less Crowd." Immediately they decided to break from that crowd and go back to Jerusalem to find Jesus.

They decided to leave this crowd first because the crowd was headed one way, and Mary and Joseph needed to go another. Secondly, Mary and Joseph left the crowd because finding Jesus was not the crowd's priority. Christ was not in the crowd, nor was finding Him a priority of the crowd.

When they made it back to Jerusalem they found Jesus in a very likely place—the temple. Scripture says that Jesus at the young age of twelve was talking to the wise men of that day and amazing them with His knowledge and conversation. They had never heard a child speak like that child. They had never seen a child behave like that child. What these learned men were not aware of was that this child was not begotten of man but by the Spirit of God. Scripture says that the Holy Spirit overshadowed his mother Mary, and she conceived a child that would be called the Son of God (Luke 1:35). This child came to save His people from their sins, (Matthew 1:21). This child came that we might have life and have it more abundantly, (John 10:10).

When Joseph and Mary scolded Jesus for staying behind, Jesus reminded them that He was to be about His Father's business, (Luke 2:49).

It is time that we as children of God make the determination to be about our Father's business. Once you receive Christ, old things are passed away and all things become new, (II Corinthians 5:17). This new life in Christ requires that we "...walk circumspectly, not as fools, but as wise..." (Ephesians 5:15). We must be very careful about those with whom we associate. Ask God to show you to whom you should draw closer and from whom you should move away. Surround yourself with those individuals who will encourage you in your commitment to live in accordance with the will of God for your life. In so doing, you will receive the support needed to grow in grace and in the knowledge of Jesus Christ, and live a life that is pleasing to the Father. Never forget to check your crowd.

THE WOLF COUNTRY

"Behold, I send you forth as sheep in the midst of wolves: be ye therefore wise as serpents, and harmless as doves."

Matthew 10:16

One evening while I was at home watching television with all four of my children, we saw an episode of the television show "Grizzly Adams." In this episode, a young woman was trying to find her lost brother. Her brother had gone off into the wilderness and had not been seen or heard from since. The young woman sought help from Grizzly Adams because of his familiarity with the wilderness and because of his knowledge of that region. She said, "I'm looking for my brother and I've been told that you could direct me to a trail that would take me into the depths of the wilderness where my brother was last seen." Grizzly Adams attempted to discourage this young woman and told her, "I admire what you are trying to do. I think it's admirable that you are looking for your lost brother, but I want to tell you that wolves inhabit the part of the wilderness that you are talking about and you don't need to be in the wolf country! There are ravenous, bloodthirsty wolves there, who have been known to literally tear people apart." So he told her, "Please stay out of the wolf country." That gave me the idea as to what to title this message: "The Wolf Country."

The tenth chapter of the gospel according to Matthew describes a meeting between Jesus and His twelve disciples. It's been a blessed meeting. I submit to you that it has been a good meeting by virtue of the fact that Jesus was in the midst. It's good to meet with the Lord. I must encourage you to do all you can to meet with Jesus. Whenever I meet with Him, I leave with something that I didn't have before the meeting. During my meetings with Jesus, I receive encouragement and guidance. When I set aside time to meet with the Lord, I experience unspeakable joy and peace that surpasses all understanding. So many people are in the ruts of depression and despair because they missed some meetings with Jesus. The Savior says, "Come unto me, all ye that labour and are heavy laden, and I will give you rest. Take my yoke upon you, and learn of me…and ye shall find rest unto your souls" (Matthew 11:28-29).

During this particular meeting, Jesus tells his disciples many important and valuable things. If I might paraphrase the words of our Lord, He tells them, "You have been with me now for a good little spell. You've walked with me and talked with me. You've witnessed me raising the dead. Now, I want you to go out and do great works in my name." Jesus instructs His disciples to go out and tell men and women that the kingdom of Heaven is at hand. He also tells them "Heal the sick, cleanse the lepers, raise the dead, cast out devils: freely ye have received, freely give," (Matthew 10:8).

Jesus also went on to tell them that, when they come to a place, if the people don't receive them hospitably, they should leave. He said, "...when ye depart out of that house or city, shake off the dust of your feet." Jesus went on to say that it would be worse for those who reject them than it was for the land of Sodom and Gomorrah, (Matthew 10:14-15).

Now, when we arrive at this sixteenth verse, he says, "Behold." Jesus seems to issue a type of divine subpoena for their attention. A "behold" from Jesus means stop everything, look and listen to what He has to say. He says, "Behold, I send you forth as sheep in the midst of wolves." In other words, "I'm sending you forth as sheep, and I'm sending you into the midst of wolves. I'm sending you into wolf country." Notice here that He does not send them as lions in the midst of wolves. As vicious as wolves are, any wolf would think twice before attacking a lion. He does not send them out as bears in the midst of wolves but as sheep. What a contrast—sheep in the midst of wolves.

Wolves are predatory by nature. Wolves go stalking their prey, seeking whom they will devour. Wolves have sharp, razor-like fangs. If you think about it, the most dangerous part of a wolf is its mouth. They can shred the flesh from the bodies of their victims in a matter of moments. Wolves also have a growl so fierce that it can send chills down a grown man's spine.

I submit to you that in this passage of scripture, the Master was not referring to actual wolves but He was referring to a certain group of people. The Savior was describing a group of people with wolf-like tendencies. Some people can inflict so much harm and pain with their words. Their words can create deep wounds. They can harm and hurt relationships just by what they say. Scripture warns us of the impact of words by saying "Death and life are in the power of the tongue…" (Proverbs 18:21).

Wolves also have paws that are specially designed for digging. Even when their prey has gone underground, they can use their paws to dig down to where their prey is hiding. People who are wolf-like in this regard are always trying to dig up something on someone else. They want to get "the dirt" on an individual and often use that information, whether accurate or not, to defame and disgrace that individual.

Lastly, wolves usually run in packs. You may not see all of them, but all of them see you! They have keen eyesight and a tremendous sense of smell with which to track their victim. They become so skilled in their work as a pack until they encircle their prey. One goes to the right. One goes to the left. One gets behind. One gets in front, and the others disperse themselves in between so that no matter which way the prey turns, he is looking at a wolf! They encircle the prey, drawing closer and closer. The leader of the pack tells the others when to attack and it's biting time! They simultaneously attack the prey to bring the prey down.

Another thing that is even more frightening about wolf-like people is that you will not only encounter wolves out in the world, but wolves are so bold and tenacious that they will even enter the church. They will put on choir robes and usher uniforms. They will even cross their legs on the deacons' bench. I must even confess that I have caught glimpses of wolves in the pulpit.

I had a long talk with the Lord about this sheep in the midst of wolves business. I said, "Lord, if you love us like you say you do, why would you send us as sheep to face the perils of The Wolf Country? Why Lord? Why would you send those of us who have forsaken all to follow You into a situation wherein we are at such a disadvantage? It seems like a certain death sentence—a sheep against a wolf. Sheep are harmless and defenseless. Wolves are ferocious and bloodthirsty. Sheep don't have long fangs, sheep don't have sharp teeth to rip apart the flesh of others." I continued, "Lord, if you must send me out into The Wolf Country, don't send me as a sheep. If I could just have the ability to strike back, that would even the odds. Send me as a lion! Send me as a bear!"

The Lord allowed me to state my case and vent my frustration and, once I finished, He responded, "Jerry Black, you are spending too much time focusing on what the wolves have going for them. You need to focus on what the sheep have that the wolves do not."

I said, "What is that?"

The Lord replied, "Although the sheep don't growl and although the sheep don't have fangs, sharp teeth and a ravenous appetite for blood, the sheep have one thing that the wolves don't have. The sheep have a Shepherd!"

The Lord wants us to go out into the midst of the wolf country, not depending on our own power but depending on the Shepherd! Whenever you have a problem, take it to the Shepherd! He specializes in dealing with our problems!

Jesus told His disciples of that day and He is telling us today that as we go out into The Wolf Country, we must possess two characteristics. First of all, we must be wise as serpents. God's sheep must have godly wisdom. Ignorant sheep will mess up the flock. No matter what school you may have matriculated through, if you don't know God, you're not wise! It makes no difference how many degrees you may have obtained. If you don't know God, you're educated but not wise! We are instructed in scripture, "If any of you lack wisdom, let him ask of God, that giveth to all men liberally, and upbraideth not; and it shall be given him," (James 1:5). True wisdom comes from God. In order to live victoriously in The Wolf Country you have to be wise.

Secondly, He tells His disciples to be as harmless as doves. Doves are harmless creatures that, because of their calm nature, often symbolize peace. Doves don't have the ability to run, but they do have the ability to fly! Doves can go up to a higher level! When you're in The Wolf Country, don't stoop to the level of the wolf! When you're in The Wolf Country, don't do what the wolves do! When you're in The Wolf Country, rise to another level! If you stay with the Lord in The Wolf Country, He will give you power to rise to a higher level! The things that used to get you down can't bother you because you are soaring at a higher level! During a time of great distress brought on by his enemies, David said, "Oh that I had wings like a dove! for then would I fly away, and be at rest," (Psalms 55:6)

As children of God, we will at times get tired and weary in The Wolf Country. We will get tired of being growled at! We will get tired of ducking and dodging! But we must look to The Good Shepherd, who is Jesus Christ, as our refuge and guide. He alone is able to guide and comfort us as we deal with one wolf after another. With the aid of His precious Holy Spirit, God will expose the hidden agendas and ulterior motives of our enemies.

Even in the wolf country, God will walk with you, and He'll wrap His arms around you so the Devil can't do you any harm! The songwriter wrote,

> *"Be not dismayed, whatever be tide.*
> *God will take care of you!*
> *Beneath his wings of love abide.*
> *God will take care of you!"*

He promised never to leave you alone in The Wolf Country. In the time of difficulty, He will be your friend. The Word of God instructs us to humble ourselves and cast all of our cares on God because He cares for us (I Peter 5:6-8). The hymn writer describes the beauty of being totally reliant on God when he wrote:

"What a friend we have in Jesus!
All our sins and griefs to bear.
What a privilege it is to carry everything to God in prayer!"

The hymn writer goes on to say:

"Have we trials and temptations?" (That's wolves!)
"Is there trouble anywhere?" (That's more wolves!)
"Jesus knows our every weakness.
Take it to the Lord in prayer."

GOING TO ANOTHER LEVEL

"And a certain woman, which had an issue of blood twelve years, And had suffered many things of many physicians, and had spent all that she had, and was nothing bettered, but rather grew worse, When she had heard of Jesus, came in the press behind, and touched his garment. For she said, If I may touch but his clothes, I shall be whole. And straightway the fountain of her blood was dried up; and she felt in her body that she was healed of that plague."

Mark 5:25-29 KJV

Let's examine the plight of the woman in our text. She has agonized with the same debilitating disorder for twelve long years. The record states that she has sought help from various physicians and no doubt endured painful medical procedures that, rather than improving her condition, made her condition worse. Imagine for a moment how her hopes blazed high on each occasion when she went to various physicians believing for a cure only to be disappointed time after time. Prolonged illness can be devastating. Many times, illnesses of lengthy duration can cause the sufferer to feel as if the situation will never change. Pain that persists over a long period of time can breed a sense of hopelessness and despair that takes a great toll on one's ability to see beyond the current crisis. When you've been sick for a long time, visitors grow few. People who once came to see you don't come by as often. In some instances, visitations stop altogether.

Mark refers to her illness as "an issue of blood." Scholars suggest that this condition may have been menstrual in nature causing her to be ritually unclean (Leviticus 15:25-27). This condition excluded her from all social contact with other Jews. This woman, along with all others who were considered unclean, couldn't even enjoy the privilege of worshipping in the synagogue. This made the burden of her illness even greater because, not only was she weak and in great physical pain, but she was also an outcast. She desperately desired healing but she knew that, according to Jewish law, to touch Jesus directly would have made Him unclean as well. That may be the reason for the statement, "If I may touch but His clothes, I shall be whole." Not desiring to defile Jesus, she decided to limit her contact with Him to only the edge, or hem, of His garment (Luke 8:44).

In the midst of her misery, she decides that she's going to do something. She has assessed her circumstances and no doubt thought to herself, "For twelve years I've been in this same rut.

For twelve years I have agonized with this same plague. For twelve years, I've been at this same level. I've grown weary in this rut of despair and suffering and I'm going to another level."

Her commitment to improving her physical condition should be the determination of every believer to improve his or her spiritual condition. We should desire progression in our spiritual walk. Each of us should aspire to go to a higher spiritual level than where we are now. Regardless of the knowledge that we may have obtained as it relates to spiritual matters, we should all strive to ascend to a higher level. We should all have the desire to go to another level for a number of reasons. We ought to want to move to another level first of all because to remain at the same level is an indication that there has been no growth. Children of God ought to want to get better. I thank God for how far He has brought me. I've come a long way from where I used to be, but I am constantly reminded by the Holy Spirit that I'm not all that I need to be.

> **Each of us should aspire to go to a higher spiritual level than where we are now.**

I'm reminded of a true story of three mountain climbers who were preparing to climb Mount Everest. The story of the climb became a media event. Reporters surrounded the climbers and one of them asked a very interesting, yet simple, question. The reporter asked, "With all of the inherent risks associated with this activity, why do you choose to do it?" The response to this question caused me to throw up both of my hands. One of the climbers spoke for the group. He said, "The reason we climb mountains is because we are seeking a better view." He went on to say, "We can see things better at a higher elevation than we can down here in the valley."

So many people can't see what they need to see because they are in the valley. They are trapped in the ruts of low-level thinking. So many people make costly, life-altering mistakes because they cannot see a way out of their current circumstances. For example, some have hastily chosen the wrong mate because they allowed their own desperation to cloud their vision. Many Christians choose career paths that are not in line with God's will for their lives because they can see only the world's system as their source rather than God. Many Christians have even resorted to illegal and often immoral business practices to make their living because they are unable to see the value of doing things God's way. Christians should strive to move higher in the Lord in order to seek God's excellent way. God has some things that He wants to show us but in order to see them we must go to a higher level in Him.

> **Christians should strive to move higher in the Lord in order to seek God's excellent way.**

At the height of her suffering, the woman learns that there is a new doctor in town who practices medicine in a strange fashion. She hears that this doctor can cure without the use of scalpel or stitch. She heard that this doctor could heal without herbs, drugs or potions. In fact, she heard that this doctor, himself, was medication.

The fact that she heard about Jesus is an indication that somebody was talking "Jesus talk." We engage in "Jesus talk" when we share the goodness of Jesus with others. When we tell others about His saving grace and His healing power, we are talking "Jesus talk." You never know how someone's life can be changed for the better as a result of hearing "Jesus talk." When she heard about Jesus, this woman realized that there was still hope for her. There was still a way out. Earthly doctors had let her down but things would be different with Jesus. She decided that an encounter with Jesus was what she needed to go to another level.

Determined to find Jesus, she takes to the streets. It's good to know that if you sincerely seek Him, the Master can be found. The prophet Isaiah issues this commandment: "Seek ye the LORD while he may be found, call ye upon him while he is near," (Isaiah 55:6). Sincerely seeking God is never a wasted effort, for the Word of God assures us that God rewards those who diligently seek Him, (Hebrews 11:6).

The woman is so motivated by her desire to go higher that she leaves her home and travels up the road through a great crowd seeking her miracle. She decides to leave where she is so she can go to where Jesus is. This should tell us something else about moving to another height or level in God. If you want to move to another level in your walk with the Lord, it's not good enough to simply want to do it. Moving to another level requires personal effort. Developing in the area of godly character is not something that happens instantly. Gaining a godly perspective on life does not happen overnight. These things come as a result of devoting oneself to prayer, meditation and study. Most importantly, we increase in godly character and gain godly perspective by examining the choices that we make each day. Moving to a higher level in God requires that we make the conscious decision to do things according to God's will rather than our own way.

This woman's determination paid off. She found Jesus. Unlike some of the other scriptural accounts of Jesus' ministry, on this occasion she did not find Him at church. She found Him in the streets. Jesus' presence is not limited to the church house. Our Lord cannot be bottled up in the church. He's everywhere and His power is able to operate anywhere. Jesus was on His way to Jairus' house to heal his sick daughter. When the woman caught up with Jesus, He was surrounded by a great multitude.

You can't really appreciate the situation unless you have some degree of imagination. With the aid of my spiritual imagination, I can see the woman hobbling through the streets. I wonder sometimes about her posture. When you're in pain, it's difficult to be well poised. When you're in pain, it's hard to keep proper posture, but she makes her way as best she can. She is extremely weak and, every time a sharp pain shoots through her frail body, she entertains thoughts of turning back. I would imagine that every now and then she has to encourage herself. At her weakest moment along this journey she might have said, "This journey toward Jesus is difficult and painful, but I must go. I have lived at this same level long enough. I have nothing to lose and so much to gain. I have to go to another level."

She makes it to the rear of the crowd. This is where she encounters the most difficult of obstacles. At this point in her journey, her greatest hindrance to her deliverance was the crowd. A great many people are between her and her breakthrough. I think I ought to tell you that if you are going to move higher in God, you are going to have to deal with some people. Sometimes friends won't understand. Sometimes loved ones won't believe that our situations can change. It may be that sometimes, even those dearest to us will become jealous and try to discourage or sabotage our progress. It is during these times that we must remain steadfast in our resolve rise to the new level that God has for us.

In spite of the opposition, she continues her pursuit of our Lord. She negotiates her way through the crowd until she is finally close enough to touch His garment. Scripture says, "... straightway the fountain of her blood dried up..." Jesus stops His journey and asks who touched Him. According to Mark, when the woman identifies herself as the one who touched Him, Jesus said, "Daughter, thy faith hath made thee whole; go in peace, and be whole of thy plague," (Mark 5:34).

Many leave the story at this point, but my imagination takes me back home with her. I can see her as she walks along the road, well and delivered. Her walk turns into a skip. Her skip turns into a dance. She left home sick, but she's going back well. She left home weak, but now she has renewed strength. She has endured severe pain and overcome difficult obstacles to reach her next level.

> **God's desire is that we move higher and higher in Him.**

We serve a righteous God who accepts us as we are, but loves us too much to leave us where we are. God's desire is that we move higher and higher in Him. His desire is that we "…grow in grace and in the knowledge of our Lord and Savior Jesus Christ…" (2 Peter 3:18). God has a destiny for all of our lives that requires us to ascend to higher and higher levels in Him. Why wait to only experience God's goodness in heaven when He has made so much available to us now?

Part Four:

The *Must* of Embracing Our God-Given Destinies

Introduction

"...who knoweth whether thou art come to the kingdom for such a time as this?"

Esther 4:14

No one is here by accident. I am convinced that God created every person for a purpose. This view is well supported by both Old and New Testament Scripture. God created Moses for the purpose of leading the children of Israel out of Egypt into the Land of Promise. Queen Esther's destiny was to save her people from certain destruction. The Apostle Paul was used as God's messenger to the Gentile world. Jesus came into the earth to reconcile man back to God.

God has a purpose for every life. This purpose goes far beyond salvation. God's purpose for every life even surpasses our submission to the transforming work of the Holy Spirit within our own minds and hearts. I often share with people the fact that God does not save us to sit; He saves us to serve. After receiving salvation through the Lord Jesus Christ and being given the grace to apply godly principles to our lives, we experience true liberty in Christ. This freedom, however, is not intended to only benefit us. The word of God instructs us to use this liberty to "…by love serve one another," (Galatians 5:14). Every person has a role to play in accomplishing the will of God in the earth. Our responsibility is simply allowing God to choose where and how we will serve in His Kingdom.

God-ordained service is not reserved to members of the clergy. We are all called to accomplish a specific task at a given point in time that was ordained by God from the beginning. God also equips us with special talents, gifts and abilities that will facilitate the accomplishment of these tasks. Our Heavenly Father goes even further by strategically positioning us within the Body of Christ in such a way that our service will be most effective. This often requires us to move outside of our comfort zones. We may be called to do something in God's service for which we feel completely unprepared and unqualified. We may even struggle with feelings of unworthiness and inadequacy. But children of God should receive comfort and assurance from the Word of God. Scripture states that God's strength is made perfect in our weakness, (II Corinthians 12:9). We serve a faithful God who will meet us at the point of our weakness and make the needed difference between where we are and where we need to be.

THE RACE THAT IS SET BEFORE US

"Wherefore seeing we also are compassed about with so great a cloud of witnesses, let us lay aside every weight, and the sin, which doth so easily beset *us*, and let us run with patience the race that is set before us."

Hebrews 12:1

While the author of the book of Hebrews is not known with certainty, scholars speculate that possibly the Apostle Paul wrote it. Throughout the book of Hebrews, the writer affirms the supremacy of Christ and encourages the believers of that day and even today to hold fast to their faith. The first several chapters of Hebrews establish Jesus' superiority over the Jewish high priest (Hebrews 4:14-15), Moses (Hebrews 3:1-6) and even the angels (Hebrews 1). The writer of Hebrews also affirms the superiority of the "new covenant" that was ushered in by the coming of Christ (Hebrews 8).

Just like today, the saints of that time were under tremendous pressure to turn away from their faith. In the midst of the pressure and persecution, the writer of Hebrews warns the saints to remain all the more committed to the things they had learned to avoid drifting away (Hebrews 2:1). The writer, moreover, emphasizes the importance of doing away with anything that hinders our relationship with God and looking to Jesus as the supreme example of how to withstand persecution and ultimately be victorious (Hebrews 12:1-3).

The writer begins the twelfth chapter by saying, "Wherefore seeing we also are compassed about with so great a cloud of witnesses..." Many biblical scholars are of the opinion that the writer is referring to a host of spectators consisting of those believers who came before us and are now in heaven watching with lively interest and lending heavenly aid. Still others believe that the "cloud of witnesses" is not referring to spectators, but testifiers. Those who have borne witness to the truth of God's promises are believed by some to comprise a great "cloud of witnesses." In this scenario, these champions of the faith are not actually observing events on earth, but it is their perseverance, faith and ultimate victory that should serve as encouragement to present-day saints. Regardless of the interpretation you embrace, the underlying notion inherent in both views is that present-day Christians are united with the saints of old to make up one body of believers. We are part of a holy lineage and a strong heritage of faith. If so many saints of God were able to endure hardship, disappointment and tribulation and hold fast to the faith, shouldn't we be encouraged that we also can run this race victoriously?

> **We are part of a holy lineage and a strong heritage of faith.**

The writer of our text suggests that since we are spiritual descendants of a holy nation, we must endeavor to successfully run the race that has been set before us. Permit me to emphasize the fact that the children of God have a race that is already set before them. God has a specific plan and purpose for all of our lives. In Jeremiah 29:11, the Lord states, "For I know the thoughts that I think toward you, saith the LORD, thoughts of peace, and not of evil, to give you an expected end." We cannot determine the call on our lives. The purpose for each of our lives has been divinely ordained of God and cannot be changed. The psalmist David explains, "The steps of a good man are ordered by the LORD..." (Psalm 37:23). God's will for your life is not subject to your opinion or personal desire. Likewise, God's will for your life is not affected by anyone else's opinion of you. We can, however, choose to go against God's plan and go our own way. To do so, however, would take us outside of the plan of God and set us on a path leading to frustration, discontent and possibly even destruction.

In order to achieve the will of God for our lives, the writer cautions, "...let us lay aside every weight, and the sin which doth so easily beset us…" In this statement, he implies that we all have some things that we should lay aside. We all have some obstacles to overcome. The believer must, however, put forth some effort. There are some things that God isn't going to take from us; we must rid ourselves of them by laying them aside. It seems that it would be far simpler if, upon seeing something in our character that God does not like, He would just take it away. But God wants to get us to the point where we can readily identify aspects of our lifestyles and character that are slowing us down. After we recognize these hindrances, God wants us to turn from them and say, "If this is going to hinder my relationship with God, I don't want it. I don't want anything in my life that is going to move me outside of His will." Our love for God and desire to see His will manifested in our lives should serve as motivation to turn away from anything that does not please Him. When we make the conscious decision to surrender our will to God's, then God, by His Holy Spirit, will intervene and empower us to be freed.

Many Christians think that some weights are all right to hold on to because they are not cardinal sins. If it is not adultery, fornication, murder or the like, some think that it is all right. This is not true. Some people carry the weight of gossip. They have a peculiar attraction to the intimate details of other people's lives. They travel in gossip circles because they gain a strange sense of pleasure from the pain of other people. While rejoicing in someone else's pain may not be considered to be as bad as other sins, children of God must resist this temptation because not only does it bring harm to others but it also brings dishonor to the faith that we profess. Keep in mind that gossip takes on a whole different complexion once we become the subject.

> **God doesn't give us the luxury of holding on to anything that hinders our relationship with Him.**

God doesn't give us the luxury of holding on to anything that hinders our relationship with Him. The writer specifies, "lay aside every weight, and the sin, which doth so easily beset us." We all have temptations to which we succumb with ease. So, the writer instructs the believer to release those things that so easily cause us to stumble. He assures us that once we do; we can run with patience the race that is set before us.

Why is patience necessary? Going after the things of God is not without its challenges. A tremendous internal war is waged in the heart of every person who decides to follow Jesus. In fact, each time a child of God has the opportunity to do what is pleasing to God, there is tremendous internal conflict that must be overcome. The believer desires to do the will of God, but the character traits of their old sinful nature such as pride, lust, greed, envy, jealousy, etc., often surface. The apostle Paul describes it this way, "For I know that in me that is, in my flesh, dwelleth no good thing: for to will is present with me; but how to perform that which is good I find not. For the good that I would I do not: but the evil which I would not, that I do. Now if I do that I would not, it is no more I that do it, but sin that dwelleth in me. I find then a law, that, when I would do good, evil is present with me," (Romans 7:18-21). I came to realize that, if we are going to be victorious, we must have patience. Laying aside some things will not come easily. New Christians are often intimidated by those who have been walking with the Lord for a long time. Many times, the more seasoned saints contribute to this feeling of intimidation by making newer Christians feel as if doing the will of God is easy. The fact of the matter is that even the most experienced Christian misses the mark sometimes.

This Christian race, however, is different from earthly races. In earthly races, the emphasis is placed on speed. So, to win an earthly race, you must be the fastest runner. In the Christian race, however, we are not in competition with anyone. We don't have to concern ourselves with being better than anyone else, because we are all on the same team operating under the same agenda. We are victorious if we simply complete the course. If someone else is more knowledgeable, talented or gifted at a given task, just say, "God Bless you!" and wave them on.

I am reminded of a story that appeared in the Reader's Digest some years ago. The story was about a great race where runners from across the nation went to a particular city to compete. Numbered amongst the participants was a man well into his eighties. The other runners were much younger than he and, by all indications, there was no chance that he would cross the finish line first. The article described how his fellow competitors and onlookers alike were puzzled by his desire to even participate. They wondered why he was even in the race. What these people failed to realize was that his objective was different from theirs. His goal was to run the course and make it to the finish line. His desire was to endure to the end. Success for him was simply in finishing the race regardless of how many ran faster than he.

Every child of God should have the same determination. We must commit to being runners in the greatest race of our lives. Everyone's race will not be the same but the goal for each of us is the same. In every thing we do, we must do so with a single objective—to glorify God. We must strive to honor God with our very lives. We can't run anyone else's race. We don't have to be better than anyone else. We must simply finish the course of the race that is set before us.

THE ALMIGHTY GOD

"And when Abram was ninety years old and nine, the LORD appeared to Abram, and said unto him, I am The Almighty God; walk before me, and be thou perfect. And I will make my covenant between me and thee, and will multiply thee exceedingly."

Genesis 17:1-2

What a wonderful privilege it is to be a child of God! In spite of our sins and shortcomings, in spite of our faults and failures, when we accepted Jesus Christ as Savior, we became Children of the Most High God. The apostle John conveys the magnitude of this reality by writing, "Behold, what manner of love the Father hath bestowed upon us, that we should be called the sons of God…" (I John 3:1). When you are a child of God, you are a child of Him who is the most powerful force in the universe.

So many Christians take salvation for granted. Rather than taking their instruction from the Word of God and the guidance of His Holy Spirit, they take their direction from the world. It troubles me when those who profess to be Christians blend so easily with the world and behave in the same manner as those who don't know Christ. God's desire, however, is that we conduct ourselves each day with an acute awareness of who we are and whom we serve.

Our Heavenly Father possesses many attributes that place Him in a category all by Himself. Our God is first **omniscient**. He knows all of our thoughts, words and deeds. God knows everything about us—both good and bad. In the 139th Psalm, David writes, "Thou knowest my downsitting and mine uprising, thou understandest my thought afar off," (Psalm 139:2). This is why it is useless to try to hide anything from God. Excuses about our shortcomings may work with man, but not with God.

Our God is also **omnipresent**. He is everywhere at the same time. He's where we want Him to be and He is where we don't want Him to be. Also in Psalm 139, David asks, "Whither shall I go from thy spirit? or whither shall I flee from thy presence?" (Psalm 139:7) He goes on to write, "If I ascend up into heaven, thou art there: if I make my bed in hell, behold, thou art there. If I take the wings of the morning, and dwell in the uttermost parts of the sea; even there shall thy hand lead me, and thy right hand shall hold me," (Psalm 139:8-10). This passage assures us that, no matter where we go, we are never out of God's reach or away from His comforting presence.

Lastly, and most importantly, our God is **omnipotent**. He is all-powerful. There's a portion of Genesis 17:1 that literally sends shock waves through me. It reads, "*I am The Almighty God.*" Notice that this statement is not a man's assessment of God, but it is God making reference to Himself. I receive great comfort and confidence from knowing that my Heavenly Father is all-powerful. Knowing that my Heavenly Father is almighty enables me to view my problems from a totally different perspective. I know that there is no problem that He is not able to solve. There is no distress or situation in life that my Heavenly Father cannot resolve. As a result, I can stand boldly and face any situation and any person with confidence, because I know my God can do anything but fail. I can march into my future knowing that no circumstance is too hard for Him to handle.

> **Knowing that my Heavenly Father is almighty enables me to view my problems from a totally different perspective.**

Our confidence in the all-sufficient power of God is constantly under attack. The circumstances of life can sometimes cause our faith to falter. It is during these times that the enemy bombards our thoughts. He will try to get us to turn from God by saying things like, "Yes God is powerful, but you've got a situation that's unique. Your problem is so difficult that mere faith in God will not bring about a solution." Let me encourage you that there's nothing distressing you that the Almighty God can't handle. His promises are true and His will for our lives is perfect. In the face of adversity, how can you lay hold of God's promises and fulfill His divine will for your life? You must trust in the wisdom and power of God.

> **You have to trust Him even when you can't trace Him.**

You have to trust Him even when you can't trace Him. Man is not able to fully comprehend God's ways. In Isaiah 55:8, God states, "For my thoughts are not your thoughts, neither are your ways my ways." There will be times in life when you can't trace God and when you can't fully comprehend what He's doing. This is why faith is essential. God doesn't always operate according to our timetable. The old church saying, "He may not come when you want Him but He's always on time," still encourages the hearts of believers today. There are those who would have us to believe that, because we are children of God, we are able to move the hand of God according to our own way and our own timing. This is not always true. The wisdom of God is such that He masterfully orchestrates the events of our lives (both good and bad) in such a way that they work together for our benefit. So whether His coming is sooner or later, I have resigned in my own heart that His coming is well worth the wait.

God promised Abraham, originally named Abram, a son with his wife, Sarah, originally named Sarai. Scripture says that upon hearing God's promise, Abraham believed that what God said would come to pass. Genesis 15:6 states that his faith was "counted to him for righteousness." What a statement! Abraham had lived a godly life and observed God's laws for many years, but it was his faith that confirmed his righteousness. Abraham left his father's household and his homeland at God's command (Genesis 12:1-4). Under God's direction, Abraham packed up all of his possessions and went from one region to the next, not knowing what he might encounter or where he might end up. When he and his nephew Lot parted company, he unselfishly gave Lot the choice land while he took the lesser. At a later time, Abraham rescued Lot and several others from the hands of four evil kings (Genesis 14:8-16). He even gave a tenth of his possessions as a gift to King Melchizedek (Genesis 14:18-20). Yet, despite all of his good works, it was his faith that was credited to him as righteousness. Abraham's righteousness was a direct result of his faith, not his works.

Abraham was a man of great faith, but, when his faith in God's promise for a son was tested, he disappointed God. God spoke this promise to Abraham when he was about seventy-five years old and Sarah was sixty-five, and well pass childbearing age. Abraham and Sarah remained childless for more than ten years after receiving God's promise. It was at that point that they made a mistake that nearly destroyed their family. Sarah convinced Abraham to sleep with her maidservant, Hagar, in order to realize their dream of a son. This was a common practice during that time. In that culture during that time period, for a married woman to be childless was a disgrace. Many times, it was necessary to give a female servant to the husband in order to produce an heir. According to the custom of that time, the child that resulted was considered the child of the wife.

This practice, however common it may have been, was not the will of God for Abraham and Sarah. Abraham and Sarah made the costly mistake of pursuing the fulfillment of God's promise using a worldly solution. The world's way of doing things is not God's way and engaging in worldly behavior takes us out of the will of God for our lives. Children of God must be careful not to pursue a godly end using ungodly means. If God has made a promise to you, you don't have to resort to worldly tactics in order to lay hold of it. God is not so limited in His ability to bless His children that He needs the world's help.

> **Children of God must be careful not to pursue a godly end using ungodly means.**

Rather than staying on the main highway of God's will for their lives, Abraham and Sarah chose an ungodly side road. God had promised Abraham that he and his wife Sarah would have a son. All Abraham had to do was trust God enough to stay on the main highway, which was Sarah. Even though Abraham let God down, God reaffirms His original covenant with Abraham. God comes back to Abraham in spite of his mistake. Abraham still had to deal with the consequences of his actions, with the conflict between Hagar and Sarah and the troubled life of his son Ishmael (born to Hagar), but God eventually kept His promise to Abraham. Abraham is still regarded as the "father of many nations" and the entire world has been blessed through him.

There have been times in all our lives when we've disappointed God. I don't consider myself flawless. I'm not one who has never made a mistake. There have been times when I know that I let God down. But I am so glad that in spite of our mistakes and shortcomings, God still has a plan for us. God's plan for our lives can still be achieved despite our mistakes. We don't have to be perfect to fulfill our God-given destiny—just available to the precious Almighty God.

COPING WITH THE CUP

"Then cometh Jesus with them unto a place called Gethsemane, and saith unto the disciples, Sit ye here, while I go and pray yonder. And he took with him Peter and the two sons of Zebedee, and began to be sorrowful and very heavy. Then said he unto them, My soul is exceeding sorrowful, even unto death: tarry ye here, and watch with me. And he went a little farther, and fell on his face, and prayed, saying, O my Father, if it be possible, let this cup pass from me: nevertheless not as I will, but as thou wilt."

Matthew 26:36-39

Through the window of scripture, we've seen our Lord and Savior, Jesus Christ, in a variety of circumstances. We've seen Him exhibit strong emotions, for Jesus was not devoid of emotion. We've seen Him shedding tears outside of Lazarus' tomb; hence the shortest verse in Bible, "Jesus wept," (John 11:35). We have seen Him being forceful and direct in a confrontation with Satan. When Jesus was tempted by Satan in the wilderness, He didn't try to negotiate or reason with His enemy. Jesus simply stated, "Get thee behind me Satan," (Luke 4:8). We have also seen Him become enraged over the misuse of His Father's house. Scripture says that He turned over the tables of the moneychangers and ran out those who defiled His Father's house. Jesus rebuked them saying, "It is written, my house shall be called the house of prayer; but ye have made it a den of thieves" (Matthew 21:13).

Although we've seen Him become emotional on numerous occasions, we've never before seen Him as we do now. Jesus is distraught! Jesus, who had solved the problems of countless others, was greatly distressed by a personal problem. What caused our Savior's anguish? It was a **cup**. He was greatly disturbed, heavily burdened and deeply saddened by a **cup**. A cup has caused Jesus such distress that He pleads with his Father for relief saying, "*…let this cup pass from me….*"

Permit me to say that in this context the word "cup" is not referring to that common vessel from which we drink. Instead, the word "cup" is used here to denote the unpleasant circumstances, the difficult situations and agonizing crises that often accompany a commitment to fulfilling the will of God. This may be a disturbing message for some because there are those in the Body of Christ that would have you to believe that doing the will of God is easy. Some in the Body of Christ would have many to think that pursuing God's will is effortless and trouble-free. This message is not intended to disappoint anyone or place me at odds with anyone else's teachings, but I must issue this warning: There is an uncomfortable, sometimes altogether unpleasant, side to serving God. Every child of God will have to deal with a cup and some of these cups will be extremely bitter. Even Jesus had to cope with a grievous situation from which He wished He could escape. Think about it. If God did not excuse His own Son from the cup, you and I will not go exempt. If the Son of God had to drink from a bitter cup, then we should prepare ourselves to deal with ours.

> **There is an uncomfortable, sometimes altogether unpleasant, side to serving God.**

You'd better learn how to handle your cup or your cup will handle you! I am convinced that so many blessings have been forfeited due to the inability of some to cope with their cups. So many victories have gone unclaimed and breakthroughs unrealized because a cup caused them to stop short of the goal. Let me help you do some "cup coping."

My career as a pastor has afforded me the privilege of seeing many people come to Christ. I have shaken the hands of countless thousands who have accepted the invitation to discipleship and made a sincere commitment to live for the Lord. I have personally witnessed many new converts excitedly involve themselves in many areas of church and community service out of love for their newfound Savior. Unfortunately, all too often this excitement and commitment quickly fades away at the first sign of trouble.

Successful "cup coping" requires the courage and preparation of a soldier. Children of God must recognize that they have a cunning adversary with which to contend. We are no match for Satan. With all of man's intelligence, man cannot outsmart Satan. No matter how physically or mentally strong we become, we cannot outlast the enemy. We need heavenly help in order to stand. In the book of Ephesians, the apostle Paul encourages every believer to, "…be strong in the Lord and in the power of His might." (Ephesians 6:10). The strength that we need to be victorious against the enemy is made available through God. Paul goes on to say that in order to stand we must put on the "whole armour of God," (Ephesians 6:11). Paul describes the different parts of the armor. He describes the belt, breastplate, sword, shoes and shield. Each of these items serves to protect us from outside attacks. The helmet of salvation, however, is critical in cup coping because it guards what can make the critical difference between success and failure—the mind. The enemy often uses the power of suggestion to get us to doubt God's promises. The enemy knows that he cannot curse what God has already blessed. Satan knows that he alone cannot change what God has already ordained. Satan can, however, bombard the mind with thoughts of doubt and fear that can cause the believer to hesitate or even quit. As

> **You'd better learn how to handle your cup or your cup will handle you!**

we grow stronger in the things of God, our minds are constantly being renewed to reflect the mind of Christ. The salvation that we have received through the Lord Jesus Christ is what guards our renewed minds as a helmet protects the head of a soldier.

If you're going to make a good soldier for our Lord, you must also realize that the spiritual battlefield is similar in many ways to earthly battlefields. Soldiers on earthly battlefields aren't having a good time. They aren't having picnics. They're ducking and dodging while their enemies are shooting at them! Don't get on the spiritual battlefield and be so naive as to think that no one will shoot at you! Your enemies will shoot gossip at you! They'll shoot lies at you! They'll try and run down your good name! They will attempt to assassinate your character! I dare you to get serious about the Lord! I dare you to be more than just a robe wearer! I dare you to be more than just a clergy collar wearer! I dare you to be more than just a title wearer! Once you really get the Lord down in your heart, all HELL will come at you! Devils that you didn't even expect will rise up and try to make you turn back. Despite the many things working against you, you must possess the courage of a soldier and press your way through.

The 26th chapter of Matthew describes the final moments shared between Jesus and His disciples. The religious leaders conspired with Judas Iscariot to apprehend Jesus (Matthew 26:14-15). Jesus administered the first Holy Communion (Matthew 26:26-27). After they finished, Scripture tells us they sung a hymn and went to the Mount of Olives where the Garden of Gethsemane was located (Matthew 26:30). Several disciples accompanied Jesus to the Garden of Gethsemane. At the garden entrance, Jesus stopped all but three of His disciples and told them, " Sit ye here, while I go and pray yonder" (Matthew 26:36). Then He summoned three of His disciples, Peter, James and John to continue into the garden. After traveling a little further with His three disciples, Jesus stopped them and went further into the garden alone. I am so glad that Jesus went further. Redemption's plan would not have been secured if had he not gone further.

Come with me to that place of prayer that the Master chose in the garden. Come with me and you'll find the Master having departed from Peter, James and John before He bowed down on his knees and prayed. In order to successfully cope with your cup, you must pray. The simple, yet powerful, act of prayer allows us to invoke the power of God to guide, protect and sustain us during "cup coping." Please understand that secret prayer is important. There are things that I can tell the Father in secret that I can't say to Him with others around. I can just lay it on the line when I'm alone! The prayers and support of friends and loved ones have proven to be valuable sources of strength and comfort for me during difficult times. However, in order to deal successfully with the challenges associated with doing the will of God, I had to reach a spiritual point where I could take my cares to the Lord myself and receive the help that I need.

Jesus prayed to the Father alone and this was no ordinary prayer. The Book of Saint Luke describes it as an emotional prayer. He tells us that Jesus prayed until sweat, like drops of blood, ran down to the ground (Luke 22:44). Jesus cried out, "O my Father, if it be possible, let this cup pass from me…" (Matthew 26:39). In other words, Jesus was simply saying, "Father, if there is any other way that we can pull this thing off and get man out of the mess that he's in without my having to deal with the cross, let this cup pass."

Our Savior agonized for several reasons. He knew that He would have to endure betrayal, injustice, humiliation and excruciating physical pain. In addition, He knew that taking on the sins of the world would require Him to endure separation from His heavenly Father as He suffered. Scripture informs us, however, that He was able to endure all of this "for the joy that was set before Him," (Hebrews 12:2). In other words, Jesus was able to look beyond the pain and horror, and see the joy that would come as a result of reconciling man back to God. Hebrews 12:3 instructs the believer to "consider Him" in the midst of hardship, "…lest ye be wearied and faint in your minds."

> **Jesus was able to look beyond the pain and horror, and see the joy that would come as a result of reconciling man back to God.**

To successfully handle your cup, you must also have the spirit of a servant. Your will must be lost in the will of the Father. The record tells us that Jesus didn't end the prayer with "let this cup pass". He went on to say, "...nevertheless, not as I will but as thou wilt," (Matthew 26:39). I often tell people that our prayers must be contingent upon the Lord's will. We should say, "Lord, this is what I'm asking for, but it's conditioned upon Your will. If it meets with Your approval, let me have it. If it does not, then help me bear it.

It's natural for people to desire the removal of that which is painful. It is normal for us to want to be free of things that are distressing. But it is not always the will of God to do so. The challenges that we face often work to develop godly character and make us into vessels fit for the Master's use. Another of the synoptic gospel writers, the Apostle Luke, recorded something that Matthew didn't mention. Luke wrote that after Jesus finished praying, God dispatched an angel from Glory to the garden of Gethsemane to strengthen His Son, (Luke 22:43). God's answer to Jesus' prayer was not to deliver Him from the situation but to strengthen Him so that He could bear it. The apostle Paul had a similar experience with what he called a "thorn in the flesh." He prayed three times that this thorn would be removed but, rather than change the situation, God strengthened Paul. The Lord comforted Paul with these words: "My grace is sufficient for thee: for my strength is made perfect in weakness," (II Corinthians 12:9).

We experience God's strength more fully during our times of weakness and hardship. During our times of adversity, we become all the more dependent on the Lord rather than our own strength or our own wisdom. For this reason, Paul did not complain about his weakness. Rather, he writes, "…therefore will I rather glory in my infirmities, that the power of Christ may rest upon me. Therefore I take pleasure in infirmities, in reproaches, in necessities, in persecutions, in distresses for Christ's sake: for when I am weak, then am I strong," (II Corinthians 12:9-10).

> **We experience God's strength more fully during our times of weakness and hardship.**

I don't fight that theology that says, "God didn't call me to be a mountain climber, He called me to speak to the mountain and tell it to move." While, in some instances, this is certainly true, still there will be some difficult situations that we are going to have to deal with. Thanks be to God that He has given His children access to the strength needed to endure hardship as good soldiers. God has also made it so that the hardships that we face in His service are never in vain, and in return, we can victoriously "cope with the cup."

STILL WANTED BY THE LORD

"But go your way, tell his disciples and Peter that he goeth before you into Galilee: there shall ye see him, as he said unto you."

Mark 16:7

An angel of the Lord has given clear instructions to a small group of women, Mary Magdalene, Mary, the mother of James, and another by the name of Salome. They have been instructed to inform Christ's disciples and also Peter that Jesus will rendezvous with them in Galilee. The angel says, "...tell His disciples and Peter." Notice that the angel says nothing about James. He makes no specific mention of John, but he mentions Peter.

I became extremely interested in the fact that the angel specifically identified Peter. Peter has fallen short. Peter has missed a mark. Peter failed to stand up at a time when he should have taken a stand. As a result, Peter has fallen into the ruts of shame and despondency. Scripture says that Peter has gone into seclusion because he let Jesus down. Nevertheless, the angel very clearly states that Jesus wants to see Peter. In essence, the angel says, "Go tell the other disciples but be sure to tell Peter that Jesus wants to see them in Galilee". My heart rejoices in the fact that Jesus did not want only James and John. Jesus didn't desire to only see the other disciples, but He had a desire for the one who failed Him. He had a desire for the one who let Him down.

> **He had a desire for the one who let Him down.**

That's good news! Jesus still wanted to see Peter. I'm happy about that because there have been some occasions in my life when I've been in Peter's position. I haven't been perfect. I haven't dotted every "I" and I haven't crossed every "T"! This message from the angel at this dark hour lets us know that if Jesus had a desire to see Peter, He still wants you and me!

This occasion has followed a series of terrible events. Jesus' trial is over. His sentencing and execution on the cross have already taken place. Jesus' body has been removed from the cross and buried. All of those events that were so painful and so difficult for the Master are now over. Aren't you glad that troubles don't last always? Aren't you glad that regardless of the problems we may be experiencing right now, we can join ranks with the songwriter who said, "This too shall pass"?

According to Scripture, a glorious event has also taken place. I've said on several Easter Sunday mornings, this glorious event happened, in of all places, the graveyard. This event was so miraculous that it would forever change the image of the graveyard.

Christ has been raised from the dead. Ever since then, things have not been the same in the graveyard. I can walk into the graveyard shedding tears but I grieve not as those who have no hope, for I grieve knowing that there's a day coming when my departed loved ones and I will be together again.

Jesus was crucified, but He rose on the third day. His enemies and His foes including the Devil himself were not able to keep our Lord down. I'm glad He got up for a number of reasons. One of the reasons for which I'm most glad is that by getting up, Jesus sends a serious message to the Devil. That message is that you can't keep a child of God down! Our Lord didn't get up frail and weak, but He got up with all power in both heaven and earth. You may be experiencing a down period in your life. You may have been slapped down. You may have been knocked down but if you take time to be with God while you are down, you will rise with power that you didn't have when you went down. Your strength will be restored. Your peace will return and your spirit will be revived.

The three women of our text arrived at the tomb shortly after Christ's resurrection. They came for the purpose of anointing our Lord's body with sweet spices, but when they arrived, Jesus had already departed. When they made it to the tomb they looked in and, rather than finding the body of our Lord, they encountered a young man. He was sitting in the tomb as if he were waiting on them. He was in fact an angel who had taken leave from the streets of glory on special assignment. Permit me to paraphrase. The angel said to the women, "'You can see that He's not here. He has risen just like He said He would. But I want to give you some instructions. Go and tell His disciples *and Peter* that He'll meet up with them in Galilee."

Scripture says that they sought out the disciples but they took great care to also locate Peter. I thought about this, the Lord could have just said, "Go tell my disciples," but He didn't. Our Lord extended Peter a special invitation. "Go tell my disciples *and Peter.*" We know about Peter. Peter was the disciple who had bragged to Jesus at the Last Supper. In essence, he stated, " All of these other boys may leave you. All of these other boys may forsake you, but, Jesus, you can count on me!" When the chips are down, you'll find out whom you can count on. When difficulty becomes the theme of the hour, some folks who've said, "I'm with you," will be nowhere to be found. Peter has said, in essence, "I'm with you, Lord. You can count on me." Permit me to paraphrase Jesus' response. Jesus said, "Peter, let me tell you something. Before the cock crows twice, you're going to deny me three times," (Mark 14:30).

According to Scripture, Peter was there when Jesus was on trial. Peter was outside in the cold warming himself by a small fire. Scripture informs us that there was a young woman who had been watching Peter from a distance. Peter was being watched. Mind your behavior. Mind your conduct for you never know whose eyes are upon you. You never know who sees you! She watched him for a while. It is at this point that my imagination goes into overdrive. The young woman comes up to Peter and I can see the youthful expression on her face as she speaks to Peter. No doubt with her finger pointed, she says to him, "Weren't you one of the men who were with the man on trial?" Can't you see the squint in her eyes and can't you see the expression on her face? Peter emphatically denied ever knowing the Master.

Peter was asked again, "Weren't you one of those who were with Him?" and Peter denied Jesus with an even greater intensity. I can imagine Peter saying, "Now I done told you one time that I don't know the man!" I've concluded, however, that when you have been with Jesus, folk can tell it! You can sashay into a nightclub if you want to! Go on in there where a whole lot of shaking is going on! Go on in there where they're pouring the drinks and doing their nightlife thing, but somebody can spot you when you are a child of God. You stick out like a sore thumb! You may try to blend in, but your relationship keeps bleeding out.

When you have been with Jesus, folk can tell it!

After a while, those standing around Peter began to say, "Surely thou art one of them: for thou art a Galilaean, and thy speech agreeth thereto," (Mark 14:70). In other words, Peter's accent and manner of speech gave him away. That's when Peter went ballistic. That's when Peter blew his stack. That's when Peter, the Bible said, started to *curse and swear*. My imagination tells me some of what he told her, but the Holy Spirit tells me, "Don't write it!" But I'm pretty sure that you can fill in the blanks.

Immediately after the third denial, the rooster crowed a second time. It was at that time that Peter realized that what Jesus predicted had come to pass. Peter had denied his Lord. Peter failed to acknowledge the relationship he had with the Son of God for fear of what people would say or do. At a time when he should have stood up and owned his Lord, he coward down. When Peter realized what he had done, Scripture says, he wept bitterly.

Has there ever been a time when you had a tremendous opportunity to stand as a bold witness for Jesus and didn't? Has there even been a time when you found yourself in the company of the unsaved and hid the fact of who you are so that you might fit in? Don't judge Peter too harshly because, if honest, all of us at some point and time have been in Peter's position. You may not have openly denied Jesus with your mouth, but there have been times when your actions and conversation did not reflect your new life in Christ for fear of what others might say.

> **The Lord needs somebody who will own Him when it's not popular.**

The Lord needs somebody who will own Him when it's not popular. It's easy to go to church and shout our "Hallelujahs" and wave our hands, and dance and rejoice, but when we get out yonder into settings and situations where it is not popular to be a child of God, how do we stand? Let me tell you this, at some time in your life, your faith in the Lord is going to be tested. Your strength as a Christian is going to be put to the test. Sooner or later, you are going to have to deal with criticism from unbelievers. That unbeliever may be your supervisor. You may have a co-worker who has no use for Jesus. Before you leave this world, you will be thrust into a situation where it is unpopular to be a Christian.

The report is that on the morning of the third day, the women left the tomb with a word to deliver to the Lord's disciples but also to Peter. It was at this point that I got happy. Jesus not only wanted to see those who had continued to stand, but He wanted to see the one who had failed Him. He wanted to see that one, Peter by name, who had disowned Him. He wanted to see that one who swore he had no knowledge of Jesus.

Think about it. God still has a plan for those of us who have fallen short. God uses imperfect people to accomplish His will in the earth. Those who have let God down are still wanted by the Lord.

That's good news! Because nobody has been right all of the time! Everybody has made some mistakes along this journey! Some people try to give the false impression that they have been guiltless and sinless all of their lives. Some people within the Body of Christ would have others to believe that they have never fallen short and never made a mistake. But there are also those of us here who've lived long enough to know better.

Some of us know that on this journey everybody messes up sometimes! On this journey everybody makes some mistakes.

I rejoice in the fact that the Lord still wants me in spite of my shortcomings and in spite of all of my downfalls. The Lord still wants use me in His service in spite of the fact that I have *zigged* when I should have *zagged* and *zagged* when I should have *zigged*! The Lord still wants me and He wants you! The Lord still extends His love, His grace and His mercy toward us.

Look at us. We are saved sinners. We are saved by grace and not because of anything that we have done. The Lord picked us up when we had fallen down and gave us another chance. We are wanted by the Lord! That makes our stock mighty valuable. Nobody else may want you. Nobody else may want to even give you the time of day, but you're wanted. You're wanted by the Lord!

Part Five:

THE *MUST* OF PRAISING GOD

Introduction

What a privilege it is to be numbered among the righteous! We serve an awesome God who spared no expense to save our souls from eternal death. The guarantee of salvation would be enough to make our Heavenly Father worthy of the highest praise. Just knowing that our sins are forgiven would be sufficient to earn all glory forever, but God didn't stop at salvation. In fact, salvation was just the beginning. For this reason, children of God ought to make praising God more than an event. Praising God should be a lifestyle.

How do we make praise a lifestyle? Of course, we praise Him by singing, dancing and clapping, but we also can praise and honor God through service. Supplying the needs and uplifting the heart of someone else is a form of praising God.

True praise is also a powerful weapon in the hands of a believer. Scripture says that the Lord inhabits the praise of His people. So, when we praise God, He shows up! The presence of the Lord is ushered into the midst of difficult times and hard trials by the act of praise. There are many examples in the Bible when praise brought deliverance from danger and freedom from bondage. Don't dare limit praise to a church service!

THE REASON I LOVE HIM

"But he was wounded for our transgressions, he was bruised for our iniquities: the chastisement of our peace was upon him; and with his stripes we are healed."

Isaiah 53: 5

I am convinced that no one loves without a reason. Even when it comes to the love of God that is shed abroad in our hearts by the Holy Spirit, there is a reason. There is something within us that causes us to love even those who are not lovely and who are not lovable. If we love at all, there is a reason. It causes us to love in spite of. Something causes us to love and I'm convinced that it's not enough to say that we love Jesus; we ought to be able to intelligently share with others, by way of our own personal testimonies, the motivation behind this love affair.

One songwriter captured it so well when he wrote, "There is a name I love to hear. I love to sing its worth. It sounds like music in mine ear, the sweetest name on earth." He goes on to say in the refrain, "O, how I love Jesus. O, how I love Jesus. O, how I love Jesus." The lyricist then states the reason: "Because He first loved me."

Some time ago, I was watching a national television talk show and I never will forget one particular couple. The husband and wife were seated side-by-side on the stage and the wife was very upset. The husband had been unfaithful and the couple appeared on the show to discuss their problems. The wife was asked why she was so sure that her husband had cheated. She replied "Well, I know he has been unfaithful because, on more than one occasion, I have caught him in the very act." Maybe you saw that episode.

The wife went on to say, "I'm tired. I've been faithful to him. He has asked me to forgive him once before and I took him back only to be hurt again. I'm just here to tell him that we're through!" The husband went down on one knee and begged for another chance. He pleaded with his wife, "Honey, please forgive me. I love you!" I must give the brother credit. He wasn't much of a husband, but he was a good beggar! The wife turned to him and with a stern expression on her face said, "Why do you love me?" Her question stirred within me a thought that we ought to know why we love anyone. We should even know why we love the Lord.

Isaiah, who is referred to by many theologians as "The Eagle-Eyed Prophet," prophesied the coming of Christ hundreds of years before He actually arrived. No other Old Testament prophet describes Jesus in as much detail as the prophet Isaiah. Isaiah talks about Jesus as one who was not physically attractive. Isaiah 53:2 states, "...he hath no form nor comeliness; and when we shall see him, there is no beauty that we should desire him." Jesus was not one that people would follow simply because of his physical appearance. Thus, the many portraits that we see of Jesus are actually misleading. Jesus was not an attractive man. The power of Jesus was within Him and was certainly in His word.

Isaiah goes on to describe the reason we should all love Jesus. First of all, Isaiah tells us that he was wounded for our transgressions. Jesus took our place on the cross. By right, you and I had an appointment with destruction, but Jesus flipped the script! He became our substitute. Isaiah also wrote that Jesus was despised and rejected of men. In fact, He was wounded by some of the very people He came to save.

> **By right, you and I had an appointment with destruction, but Jesus flipped the script!**

I have an even greater appreciation for the Lord's Supper when I think of all that it represents. The bread symbolizes Jesus' broken and bruised body. The wine symbolizes His sinless blood that was shed for the remission of sins. When we partake of the Holy Sacraments, we do so in remembrance of the sacrifice that Jesus made to reconcile mankind back to God. Scripture does not dictate the frequency with which we should participate in this ceremony, but this act of obedience should serve as a vivid reminder that we are not our own but we are bought with a price (I Corinthians 6:20). This price was paid by Jesus the Christ—The Suffering Servant.

Satan tried to get Him to play other roles. Satan came to Him after His baptism when He was led of the Spirit into the wilderness, (Luke 4:1-13). The Tempter came to Jesus and said, in essence, "I've been watching you go through the motions of prayer. I was at the baptism the other day and I heard someone cry out, 'This is my beloved Son in whom I am well pleased.' But, if you are the Son of God, prove it to me!" Satan tried to throw the element of doubt into the picture. "If you are the Messiah, then command that these stones be turned to bread."

Now, when Satan said this to Jesus, he was speaking figuratively. By "bread" he meant material things. Satan seemed to say, "If you are going to play the role of the Messiah, then supply the material needs of the people. Be the Materialistic Messiah. Take on that role! Walk around supplying the material needs of the people." While Jesus knew that there was the reality to the material needs of man, Jesus had not come just to play that role. Jesus knew that you could feed a man, clothe a man, and shelter a man in the best of accommodations, but these things wouldn't make people better. Jesus turned down the materialistic approach. He refused to play that role.

Satan came to Him again. That's his way, you know. Scripture says that if you resist him, he'll flee from you (James 4:7). But don't think he'll stay gone. Eventually he'll return and come at you from another angle. Satan tried to tempt Jesus again by encouraging Him to throw Himself from the highest point of a temple in Jerusalem. Satan actually used Scripture! He said, "For it is written, He shall give His angels charge over thee to keep thee: and in their hands they shall bear thee up, lest at any time thou dash thy foot against a stone" (Luke 4:10-11).

I can imagine Satan enticing Jesus by saying, "All of the people who have come into Jerusalem for the feast will watch you in amazement. Stand there until you gain the attention of the masses—Greek, Jew and Roman. Stand up there and cast yourself down and show the people that you can fall from great heights and not die! And the folk will walk away saying 'Wow!' They'll go away proclaiming you as a Mystical Messiah!"

We live in a world that is caught up in mysticism. Psychics, palm readers, people who claim to talk with the dead are all promoting mysticism. They all rely on ungodly sources to provide answers and direction that only God can provide. Satan wanted Jesus to play the role of the "Mystical Messiah", but Jesus didn't go for that approach.

Satan came to Jesus on another occasion. Permit me to paraphrase, Satan said, "Come with me. I want to show you all the kingdoms of the world. I want you to see the power of Persia. I want you to see the nobility of Babylon. I want you to see the splendor of Rome and the glory of Greece! Walk with me in your mind and if you'll just bow down and worship me and just make a few short cuts. Don't worry about all of this holiness business. Just make a few adjustments. If you'll just bow down and worship me, I'll give you all of the kingdoms of the world!" Satan was trying to get Jesus to become a "Militaristic Messiah!" Satan tried to enter into secret negotiation with Jesus, but you know, you've got to know what to tell the Devil. Jesus told him, "Get behind me!"

That's where Satan belongs! Don't let him in front of you! Don't let him walk beside you! Take authority over him in the name of Jesus and make him get behind you! In other words, Jesus was telling the devil, if I were to put it in the vernacular of the young folk, "Get out of my face!"

Jesus would not embrace the materialistic approach. He would not embrace the mystical approach, nor would He embrace the militaristic approach. But in Isaiah 53:5 he did embrace another approach—The Suffering Servant. Thus Isaiah writes, "He was wounded for our transgressions. He was bruised for our iniquities." That makes it personal! That brings it home! Jesus didn't suffer and die for the people of that day and time only, but He suffered and died even for those of us who were yet to come!

Christ's sacrifice was so personal that you can really take out the word, "our" and replace it with your full name! If I were to do it, I would say that He was wounded for Jerry D. Black's transgressions. He was bruised for Jerry D. Black's iniquities. The chastisement of Jerry D. Black's peace was upon Him and with His stripes Jerry D. Black is healed!

I love Jesus because He came when humanity was on a course of destruction and there appeared to be no way out. When it looked like hell would be our eternal home, Jesus came! He occupied a human body for thirty-three years. I love Him because, for a period of time, He gave up the glory of heaven, to come down here and pay the price of redemption.

> **I love Him because, for a period of time, He gave up the glory of heaven, to come down here and pay the price of redemption.**

I love Him because He did something for me that no one and nothing else could have done! You see it took special blood to redeem my soul. The blood of goats, the blood of lambs, the blood of bullocks, pigeons and doves would not accommodate the need! It required the blood of a perfect sacrifice. During His time on earth, Jesus did not commit one sin or act of transgression! Jesus' body, therefore, manufactured blood that was untainted, untarnished and unpolluted by the virus of sin.

Judas didn't know what his role would be. He didn't know but heaven already knew that he would betray the innocent blood. Caiaphas, the high priest, and his wicked father-in-law Annas didn't know but heaven knew what their wicked and sinister roles would be. As regrettable as His suffering was, it was needed! It was necessary because without the shedding of His blood, there could be no redemption. Therefore, Jesus became the perfect sacrifice and paid the price for our sins!

Children of God should fully realize the awesome sacrifice that He made and forever bear in mind the tremendous price that He paid! Abraham, Isaac, and Jacob couldn't pull it off! Moses couldn't pull it off! David was one after God's own heart but he couldn't handle it! Their blood was already polluted by sin! Solomon, the wise, was still sinful and he couldn't do it! But Jesus came along when the world was at its lowest ebb and when human morale was at its lowest point. Then Jesus came and He paid the price!

So, I love Him not only because He was wounded and bruised for me, but I love Him also because of the stripes that He took on His own body that provide for my healing. You shouldn't stop reading there, however. He **was** wounded for our transgressions; He **was** bruised for our iniquities. But if you stop there, you stop prematurely. The rest of the verse states, "The chastisement of our peace was upon Him and with His stripes we are healed." What kind of stripes is the prophet talking about? He's talking about actual beatings! Every lash that was applied to His back was for our healing. Can't you see Him suffering just for you?

Every time the lash was applied, I can hear the Master say, "Oh!" Although it hurt Him, it helped you and me! Every time they hit Him, it would hurt Him, but it would heal you and me! There's healing available and there's power available! He's already left orders with heaven's nurses. You're going to get hurt sometimes but He's already left orders in the nurses' station in Glory.

The Reason I Love Him

I didn't appreciate this until I personally went through major surgery. With the type of surgery that I had, it was common to experience tremendous pain. Thus the doctor had told the nurse that I would likely require pain medication. Once I regained consciousness, I came from the recovery room and went to a regular room. I never will forget that an elderly nurse came in and said, "Do you need anything for pain?" For fear that they would give me a shot, I would say, "No, ma'am!" Anyone could tell by the expression on my face that I was hurting. She would come back in a little later and say, "Do you need anything for pain?" I would say, "No, ma'am." I declined the medication, but I was in terrible pain! That old nurse finally stopped and said, "Now listen. It's a known fact that your kind of surgery causes great pain and the doctor has already taken that into account. So, even before you woke up in the recovery room, the doctor stopped by the desk and left orders with us to administer to you just what you need whenever you need it."

I thought about that in the spiritual arena. Way back on Calvary, Jesus knew that there would be times when we would hurt emotionally and physically. He knew that there would be times when we would be in agony. Jesus has already left word with heaven's nurses' station! "They are going to hurt sometimes, but this is just what they will need when they experience pain. You know that old nurse told me one thing that had a sobering effect on me. She said, "No matter how much you hurt, young man, we can't give you the medication unless you call for it. We can't give you the medication unless you ask for it. Here's a buzzer. This rings at the nurses' station. If the pain gets too bad, press the button. This will alert us. We don't even have to be here in the room! If you just push this, we'll hurry down and give you something to ease your pain."

Jesus bore many stripes because He knew that we were going to need some pain medicine to heal broken hearts, wounded spirits, broken homes, broken marriages and broken friendships. He knew that we were going to need help for hurting bodies and so He took it a little while longer! No doubt He considered all that we would go through and said, "I've got to take a few more because they are going to need it."

If you're not getting help for your hurts, I can only tell you that you have not because you ask not! God gave you the privilege of prayer so that you can call Him up anytime and anywhere and tell Him what you want! So, by His stripes, we are healed! Not WERE but ARE! That means right now! There is healing available! Right now in your circumstances, in your situation and in your dismal and dark hours, there is help available!

> **So, by His stripes, we are healed! Not WERE but ARE!**

Thank you, Isaiah! In just a few words, you expressed the motivation behind my love affair with Jesus. You captured so well the reason I love Him.

THANKS IN EVERYTHING

"In every thing give thanks: for this is the will of God in Christ Jesus concerning you."

I Thessalonians 5:18

A challenging exhortation is given to us in the text. It speaks of giving thanks, not just in some things, but in everything. Think about it. Thanks in everything. The writer urges the believer to give thanks regardless of the circumstances, the situations, or the conditions in which he may find himself. Thanksgiving is not limited, saith the writer, to good things, but we must thank God in everything.

The Apostle Paul is the writer of these words to the saints in the Macedonian city of Thessalonica. On his second missionary journey, Scripture informs us that Paul traveled with a ministerial comrade by the name of Silas and started a church in the city of Thessalonica. When Paul and Silas went to Thessalonica, they dwelt with the people there until Paul found himself in mortal danger. Thus, they had to leave Thessalonica. Scripture tells us that they left Thessalonica and went to the city of Berea. Paul left Silas in Berea with another comrade, Timothy. Paul went from Berea to Athens, Greece. Paul left Athens and went to the city of Corinth, and it was in the city of Corinth, that he wrote this letter to the saints in Thessalonica.

In this letter, Paul encouraged the Thessalonians to hold fast to their faith even in the times of hardship. When the way grows hard, there is always the inclination to back down and to give up. Giving up is not a strange thought to entertain when going through hard times. During hard times, the Enemy will creep in and try to take advantage of us. He will come in and say, "You don't have to put up with this. You don't have to continue to go through this. Why not just end it right now?" The enemy will urge us to back down and to give up. Paul had obviously heard that such were the sentiments of many in the church of Thessalonica. So, he writes to them and urges them to remain steadfast in their faith in the Lord Jesus Christ.

> **I don't care how strong you are. I do not care how long you have been on the journey. All of us need to be encouraged.**

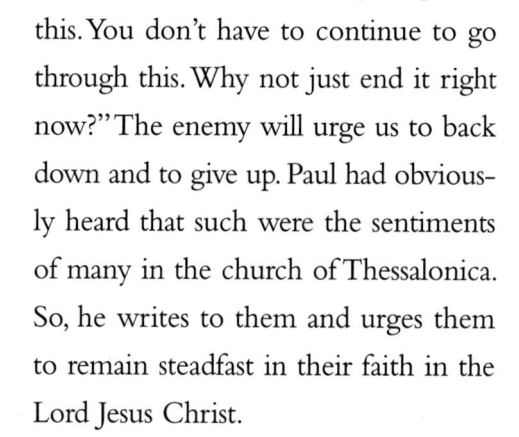

Paul writes words of encouragement to the saints at Thessalonica. Every child of God occasionally needs encouragement. I don't care how strong you are. I do not care how long you have been on the journey. All of us need to be encouraged. Paul encourages them not to grow slack in giving God thanks. Paul seems to say to the Thessalonians, "Now, even though you're experiencing hardships and difficulties, God is still God and it's just proper for children of God to give thanks."

So, Paul writes in the fifth chapter and the eighteenth verse, "In everything give thanks..." When I first read this passage of Scripture, I must confess that I had a problem with the first three words; "*In every thing.*" You see, I have discovered (perhaps you have as well) that thanking God in everything is far easier said than done.

You may ask, "Well, Paul, does that mean that if I am cursed out and called everything but a child of God, I am to still give thanks?"

Paul says, "In *every thing* give thanks."

"But, Paul, I just lost my job, and it is difficult to be in a mood of thanksgiving when I do not know where my source of livelihood shall come from?"

Paul still holds fast and says, "In *every thing* give thanks."

"Well, what if I am stricken with sickness and pain ravages my body? What if I am tossed and torn by pain and misery? Do I still give thanks?"

Paul still holds solid, "In *every thing* give thanks."

> **Our thanksgiving must not be predicated upon things going well.**

In this passage of Scripture, Paul says that our thanksgiving must not be predicated upon things going well. It is in order to rejoice when we have received some great blessing. It is in order to be jubilant when we have doors opened for us and ways made for us. But when such is not the case, it is still in order to give thanks to God. We need to realize that on this journey there are hills and valleys, highs and lows, ups and downs, good times and bad times. If our thanksgiving is contingent upon our life circumstances, we will be very inconsistent. We'll be thankful in spells, thankful in spurts, which, unfortunately, is the way a lot of Christians are. They are sporadically thankful. They are inconsistent. One day, they are saying, "Hallelujah! Praise the Lord! Thank you Jesus" but the next day it's a different story. God is still good, but you wouldn't know it by watching them. Even though God woke them up with blood still running warm in their veins, they are not rejoicing in His goodness due to their circumstances.

I am so tired of "sometimey saints!" I am so tired of saints that go from hot to cold! As children of God, we ought to arrive at the conclusion that the songwriter did, "Any way you bless me Lord, I'll be satisfied!" Things did not always go well with God's son, Paul. There were days when Paul was harshly ridiculed. There were days when he was lied on. There were a number of attempts to take his life. There were even days when he was beaten and spat upon. Nevertheless, he remained consistent in his thanksgiving and he urged his followers to do the same. Job praised God even in the midst of hard times. When his servants told him about all he had lost, Job said, "...the LORD gave, and the LORD hath taken away; blessed be the name of the LORD," (Job 1:21). In spite of the fact that our circumstances might not always be pleasant, children of God should strive for consistency in giving thanks to God, because He is consistently good to us.

Paul's words to the church are very powerful. In essence, He tells them, "You're going to have a variety of experiences as you journey through life. And there will be some things that will hurt and grieve you. There will be some people who will hurt you, who will mistreat you and who will misuse you, but don't let that rob you of your ability to give thanks to God!"

I have learned that we cannot give thanks unless we have a grateful spirit. Paul is saying that in everything we are to maintain an attitude of gratitude. In everything, we are to hold on to an appreciative spirit. We ought to appreciate God's goodness regardless of our circumstances. If we give Him thanks in everything, we will discover that we can thank and praise our way through a storm! We can thank and praise our way through trials and tribulations! We can thank and praise our way through the difficulties of life.

> **Thanking God in everything requires great faith.**

Thanking God in everything requires great faith. I thank Him even when times are rough because my faith enables me to look right over the crisis of the hour, and realize that there is a brighter day ahead. My faith allows me to say, "I am coming out of this!" By faith, I can see my deliverance and I know that my breakthrough is at hand; thus, in everything I can still give thanks. I can personally testify that God will give you "a praise" in the midst of your storm! You are able to thank Him for where you have been and thank Him for where you are because you know that, even in the rough times, all things work together for the good of those who love the Lord (Romans 8:28). If you are in it, God is going to let it work out for your good!

We have to thank God in everything also because the devil doesn't know what to make of us when we say, "Hallelujah anyhow." It drives the devil crazy. It drives him insane! The devil wants us to be in a state of depression. He wants us to be in a state of despondency and desperation. The Enemy wants the world to see Christians who don't smile and who are always depressed. Our Adversary delights in seeing Christians who are always down in the dumps, because that is a poor reflection of God! If we say, "Our Father is rich in houses and land", if we say, "The Lord will make a way somehow," if we say, "God can do anything but fail," and then every time we turn around we have a sad face and a bowed down head, it sends a bad message! If God is so able, we should get some pep in our step!

> **Our Adversary delights in seeing Christians who are always down in the dumps, because that is a poor reflection of God!**

I wish I could have been there when the church folk at Thessalonica got this letter. I can imagine that they were encouraged more and more as each line was read. As the reader spoke, they became all the more inspired. I imagine that the listeners would stop the reader at different points and say, "Can you please read that again?"

I can hear the reader say, "In everything give thanks..." He then goes on to give the most important reason why children of God should give thanks in everything, "...for this is the will of God in Christ Jesus concerning you." It is God's will that we thank Him. It is God's will that we praise Him. It is God's will that we glorify Him. It is God's will that we exalt Him. "This is the will of God in Christ Jesus concerning you."

"Lift up your heads, O ye gates; and be ye lift up, ye everlasting doors; and the King of glory shall come in. Who is this King of glory? The LORD strong and mighty, the LORD mighty in battle" (Psalm 24:7-8). With this assurance, we can say to the Lord, "Thank you for all you've done for me! The situations in my life might not always be good but You are always good."

In everything, whatever our everything is, we are to give Him thanks! In everything, whatever we are going through, whatever they are saying about us, whatever they're doing to us, we are to give Him thanks. We are to proclaim, "I'm happy and I don't care who knows it! God has been good to me, and I am going to give Him thanks."

PASSIONATE PRAISE

"I will praise thee with my whole heart before the gods will I sing praise unto thee. ² I will worship toward thy holy temple, and praise thy name for thy lovingkindness and for thy truth: for thou hast magnified thy word above all thy name."

Psalm 138:1,2

Delivered on July 21, 2002 at Beulah Missionary Baptist Church in Decatur, Georgia

The psalmist, King David, has arrived at a serious conclusion. David has come to a serious point of resolve. He has decided that he will render an offering to Jehovah. This offering will be different from standard offerings. It will not be an offering of silver or gold. This will not be a monetary offering. David concludes that he will give an offering of praise to the Lord. David has further concluded that he will not praise the Lord in some half-hearted manner. He will not praise God in some mediocre fashion. David will put all that he has into this offering of praise. He is going to praise God not with part but with his whole heart.

Wholehearted praise is passionate. We perform many tasks with a certain degree of dedication and commitment but, when you cross the line into being wholehearted, you're operating at a level of intensity, at a level of seriousness, at a level of enthusiasm that is best described as *passionate*. I want to talk about "Passionate Praise."

The Book of Psalms is highly seasoned and spiced with calls for praise. Psalms has the business of praise as its central theme and its central focus. Praise is woven into the fabric of Psalms from start to finish.

Praise is a major theme, not only in the Book of Psalms, but also throughout the entire Bible. I'm always on the look out for recurring themes. Praise is mentioned hundreds of times throughout the Bible. Since praise appears so frequently in the Bible, obviously praise is important to Jehovah.

In this day and time many church people are very concerned about finding their purpose and their rightful place in the scheme of God's will. There is great concern on the parts of many in the body of Christ regarding where they belong. Many have asked, "What am I here for?" "Now that I'm saved, what am I suppose to be doing?" "Now that I'm a member of the body of Christ, what is my purpose? What should my role be?" These are all worthy concerns. We may not know in every case all that God would have us to do. There are some things that perhaps He desires you to do that you may not yet be aware of. But there is one thing I can tell you that we are all supposed to be doing—**PRAISING GOD!**

Your role may not be that of a preacher or teacher. Your role may not be that of a pastor, deacon or trustee. Your role may not be that of an usher or choir member, but there's one thing that I know that all of us as children of God are supposed to be doing. We are supposed to be engaged in the business of praising God. That's a responsibility for each of us. That's something that all of us are required to do.

The book of Psalms ends with an urgent call and exhortation to praise. The Word says, "Let every thing that hath breath praise the Lord," (Psalm 150:6). That means that if you are breathing, you are required to praise the Lord! If there is breath in your lungs, you qualify as one who ought be engaged in the business of praising the Lord. Breathing qualifies you!

> **If you are breathing, you are required to praise the Lord!**

Passionate praise is pleasing to God. But what is praise? What is this thing called praise? If I don't know with certainty what it is, then I can't be sure that I'm doing it. Since praise is pleasing to God, I need to be sure that I'm making high marks in the praise department. What is praise? Praise is simply our expression in word or in deed that proves pleasing, honoring and glorifying to God. Praise is our expression of honor and glory to God. Praise is exalting God. Praise is lifting God.

His word says, "And I, if I be lifted up from the earth, will draw all men unto me." (John 12:32) Now, this world is lifting a lot of stuff that doesn't qualify to be one inch from the ground. *Amen.* Pornography is being lifted. Drugs are being lifted. Sexual promiscuity is being lifted. All kinds of deviant lifestyles are being promoted and lifted. Homosexuals and lesbians are lifting their agenda. They've organized parades to lift and promote their agenda. They've even come out with an annual day that they call "Coming Out Day" when gay people come out of the closet and go public with their lifestyle. Don't you know that if these groups can come out and lift their agendas, you and I as children of God have right and reason to lift the Savior up? Let me tell you something. If my "Amen" will get Him up, He's going up! If my "Hallelujah" will get Him up, He's going up! His cause will not suffer due to any lack of praise from me!

> **Praise is simply our expression in word or in deed that proves pleasing, honoring and glorifying to God.**

Why should we praise Him? First of all, we ought to praise Him because He's worthy. He's worthy. You don't have to be a Rhodes Scholar or a rocket scientist to know that God is worthy to be praised. Our Heavenly Father is both creator and sustainer of the universe. He was there before the beginning and will be there after the end. Our Lord has all power both in heaven and on earth (Matthew 28:18). His word is not subject to political authority or popular opinion. He is God and beside

Him there is none other. His wisdom is unsearchable (Romans 11:33). Mankind cannot fully possess or comprehend the infinite wisdom of God. The good news is, however, that even though we may not fully understand His ways, God's matchless wisdom perfectly orchestrates the circumstances of our lives (both good and bad) to work together for our benefit. His love toward us is perfect. His unconditional love for us was demonstrated when he sent Jesus to die for our sins (John 3:16) thereby making us His children (I John 3:1). So, He has the power to sustain us; He has the wisdom to know what is best for us; and He loves us so much that He uses that same power and that same wisdom to alter life circumstances on our behalf. Children of God ought to praise Him just for who He is.

> **Not only should we praise Him for who He is but we ought to praise Him for what He's done.**

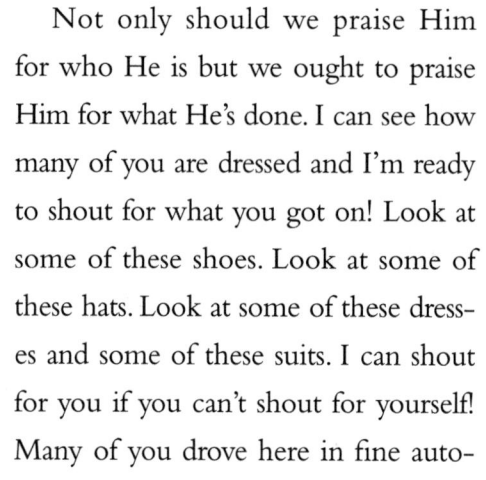

Not only should we praise Him for who He is but we ought to praise Him for what He's done. I can see how many of you are dressed and I'm ready to shout for what you got on! Look at some of these shoes. Look at some of these hats. Look at some of these dresses and some of these suits. I can shout for you if you can't shout for yourself! Many of you drove here in fine automobiles. I don't think anybody came here in a horse and buggy. I don't think there are any mules tied out back. He's worthy because of what He's done in your life and in my life.

God loves for His children to sing praises to Him. He loves for us to come before Him with uplifted voices singing praises to His name. But one must not limit praise to just singing. While it is true that singing is a part of praise, one must not limit praise to singing only. Think about it. If God limited praise to just singing, what about the folks who can't sing? What about those who sing but don't sing that well? God wouldn't leave those who are not vocally talented out of this business of praise.

God has so designed praise that anything that you do that exalts God qualifies as praise. Anything that you're involved in that brings glory and honor to God is praise. Anything that you do that extols God and advances His cause, qualifies as praise.

I've done a lot of research on Heaven. I thought I'd better find out what's going to be happening when I get there. Because you see when I get to Heaven, I'll be out of a job! There won't be any preaching there! All preaching will be over! Nobody will call me to say, "Reverend Black, will you bring the message?" In Heaven, preaching will be over! When you think about it, there won't be any deacons, ushers or missionary circles either. When we get to Heaven, a whole lot of us will be out of work!

During my study of Heaven, I've read about the golden streets. I've read about the walls of jasper. I've read about the sea of crystal and the tree in the midst of the city that has leaves good for the healing of a nation. I have also read about the great gathering around the throne. Right now in heaven there are legions of angels who do nothing but just stand around the throne praising the Lord. And around six this evening, they'll still be praising Him. At eight tonight, still praising Him. Twelve midnight tonight, still praising Him! And since there won't be any preachers, deacons, missionary circles or usher boards in heaven, what will we be doing? We are going to join this gathering around the throne and just praise His name forever. Praise will be going on when everything else has ended.

In Psalm 138, David has come to a serious conclusion. Listen to him. "*I will praise thee.*" Now, David has concluded that he is not accountable for what others do. He is only in charge of his own actions. Personally, I had to make the decision that, when it comes to praise, I can't speak for nobody else. I can only speak for Jerry Black. If nobody else does, **I** will praise the Lord!

> **Praising God doesn't have anything to do with the attitude of the person beside you.**

Thank God that praising God doesn't have anything to do with the attitude of the person beside you. I'm glad that's the case because you might be seated beside someone who came to church for everything but praising God! But that should not affect your ability to praise the Lord! Sometimes God seats you beside one of those dry bones! Sometimes God will seat you beside a dry vessel. He sometimes likes to put Ezekiels in the proximity of dry bones. Let your cup run over and maybe some of the spillage will hit that dry one sitting beside you!

David concludes, "I will praise thee!" Now you've got to conclude in your mind what **YOU** are going to do. Then you need a praise in your spirit that people can't shame you out of. You need a praise in your spirit that rises up in you to the point that you don't care who knows it. You don't care how they look at you. You don't care what they say!

I've noticed that every time somebody starts praising God, you'll always find a self-appointed "keep 'em quiet committee." Jesus was on His way into Jerusalem on Palm Sunday. There was a crowd that lined the streets. They broke off palm branches and threw them on the road and they started crying out with voices of praise, "Hosanna to the King that cometh in the name of the Lord" and there was a "keep 'em quiet committee" that showed up that day down there in Jerusalem. They said to Jesus, "Make these folk be quiet. Make them shut up." Jesus told the committee, "Now listen, if these hold their peace, I got some rocks out there that will cry out!"

Our praise must not be limited to the church house. It's expected for us to praise Him here, but we should take this praise on out there. Take it home with you and let your children see you praising God at home. Let them see you catch on fire at home! Let them know that you can't add God up like two plus two. He moves in mysterious ways and you'll never be able to totally figure Him out. Let them know that sometimes He'll touch Mama, and Mama will run when nobody's after her. Sometimes he'll touch Daddy, and Daddy will wave his hands and shout, "Hallelujah."

Now permit me to say this, the writer here has arrived at a point of passion in his praise. He says, "I'm going to put some feeling and fervor in my praise. I'm going to praise the Lord with my whole heart. I'm going to praise Him with passion." When you give Him passionate praise, the praise is so intense, until you move to another level. You step out of yourself and you're praising Him with your whole, complete and total heart. Has there ever been a time that you came through those doors and praised the Lord with your whole heart? Has there ever been a time that you came here and stopped looking at others long enough to praise God with a certain level of intensity? You praised Him with a certain degree of fervor. You praised Him with a certain degree of power.

There ought to be passion in our praise. I loved what I saw this morning when the deacons caught on fire during devotion. Scripture says that you ought to be full of the Holy Ghost and wisdom and apt to teach. Don't you know that if you're full of the Holy Ghost, He is going to have His way with you sometimes? Something is going to happen to you. You've moved beyond yourself and what's coming from you is empowered by the Lord! Let Him have His way with you! We need fiery deacons! Fiery preachers! Fiery mothers! Something ought to happen to you sometimes! Passion ought to be in our praise!

Now let me say this as I hurry to close. When Mrs. Black and I prepared to get married, (excuse this personal reference but it just drives my point home). I told her before the "I do's," that

"Honey I want you to understand that I love passion." There it is. The word is out! Now you know! I told her, "I love passion!" Don't just touch me and have no passion. When you touch me, when you rub me, do it with some passion! *Somebody here can testify!* It ain't nothing wrong with getting a passionate rub! Passion will keep your home together! It'll keep the sparks of romance alive in your marriage! Don't you know that if we want passion in our human relationships, God wants passion in our praise?

Some people just praise God when they feel good. Some only praise God when they feel like it. In Psalm 34, David says, "I will bless the Lord at ALL times." That means you ought to praise God when you feel good and when you feel bad!

Praise Him in the good times!
Praise Him in the bad times!
Praise Him when you're well!
Praise Him when you're sick!
Praise Him when you get a promotion!
Praise Him when they step on you!
Praise Him with your whole heart!

David said, "...before the gods will I sing praise unto thee." You need to read that statement carefully or you will miss what David is saying. The first letter in the word "gods" is a small "g", meaning that there will be other gods. David seems to say, "This world will have other gods but, Lord, my relationship with you will be so intense that I'll praise You even before and around other gods. While others are lifting their gods, I'm going to lift you in wholehearted praise." When I get to the job tomorrow and they're praising other things, I'm going to talk about how You blessed me at church. I'm going to talk about Your goodness and Your power and how Your Spirit moved! While they're praising houses, cars and land, I'm going to praise You, the true and living God.

As I leave you here, David goes on to tell us why. He says, "…because of your lovingkindness." He's been good to me. He's been better to me than I could have been to myself. When I think about the doors He's opened that no one else could have opened. When I think about the ways He's made that nobody else could have made. I'm going to praise Him with my whole heart because He's been good to me!

Our God is so loving and so kind that he even blesses us with things that that we haven't asked Him for. Is there anybody here who's ever been walking along and stumbled onto a blessing that you weren't even looking for? Is there anybody here who's been walking along and stumbled onto a breakthrough that you haven't even asked God for? When you praise God, He'll surprise you with blessings! Is there anybody here enjoying benefits that you weren't even expecting? He is so gracious, so loving and so kind that He rains down unexpected blessings.

Brothers and sisters, I thought about it and I got kinda' happy. Praise is a powerful thing! When you praise the Lord, God will put a hedge around you. When you praise the Lord, God will surround you with protective mercy. *Can I get a witness?*

Somebody here was in a bad condition. Someone was in a hard situation. You needed help. You needed a breakthrough, but God stepped in! God heard your cry! God answered your prayer and brought you through! Somebody else was sick and the doctor didn't think you would get well. You were sick and your body was being destroyed. You were sick and your health was going from bad to worse. But you called on the Lord and He heard your prayer! You called on the Lord and He brought you out! He healed your body! He brought you through! He saved your life!

Somebody here can testify that you needed a better place to stay. You needed a new home. *Have mercy Lord.* You tried to get that house. You tried to get that place to live and they said you'd never qualify. They said you'd never get it. But the Lord stepped in and brought you through! Now you're living at a new address. You are living at that house that God gave you! Praise His name!

When I think about the goodness of Jesus and all He's done for me, my soul shouts "Hallelujah!" Yeah! Has He been good to you? Has He been good to you? Is there a praise in this house? Is there a praise in your heart? Is there a praise in your spirit? I thank Him for His power! For His goodness! For His grace!

Now, if you can remember something that He's done for you. If you can recall a door He's opened for you. If you can remember a prayer He's answered for you or a way He's made for you. If there's a praise in your heart, will you just stop right now wherever you are and praise the Lord! Praise the Lord! Praise His name! Praise Him for His mighty acts! Praise Him for His excellent greatness! Praise Him with the string instruments and organs! Praise Him upon the high sounding cymbals! Praise Him upon the loud cymbals! Let everything that hath breath praise the Lord! Praise Him with your whole heart!

Forget about who's beside you. Forget about who's behind you. You have a right to praise the Lord! You know, in Psalm 150, when he got through saying, "Praise Him with the string instruments and organs, praise Him upon the high sounding cymbals, praise Him upon the loud cymbals", he said "praise Him with the timbrel" (that's the tambourine). And he said, "praise him with the d-a-n-c-e"! Thank you Jesus! Bless His name!